A GUIDE TO POSITIVE DISRUPTION

A GUIDE TO POSITIVE DISRUPTION

HOW TO THRIVE AND MAKE AN IMPACT IN THE CHURN OF TODAY'S CORPORATE WORLD

JOANNA MARTINEZ

LIONCREST
PUBLISHING

COPYRIGHT © 2018 JOANNA MARTINEZ

All rights reserved.

A GUIDE TO POSITIVE DISRUPTION
How to Thrive and Make an Impact in the
Churn of Today's Corporate World

ISBN   978-1-5445-1183-2 *Paperback*
　　　　978-1-5445-1184-9 *Ebook*

To Stella Leonowicz and Magali Leiseca. In their times, two exceptional disruptors.

And to Will Martinez, the great, great love of my life.

CONTENTS

INTRODUCTION

Disruption used to be a bad word. It described that kid in fourth grade who made Miss Perkins wish she had chosen another profession. Or what our houses look like the day after Thanksgiving, when the cleanup committee has failed to finish the job. Or what happens to us when our companies downsize. Our lives get disrupted.

But disruption can also be positive. Positive Disruption is change that shakes things up in a good way. Change that makes improvements, that transforms the task at hand into something very different. It is robust change that you feel.

When you're a disruptor at work, you can be a positive force for good change—the kind of change that companies need to stay alive, to thrive, to be competitive.

Over a forty-year career in business, I've experienced both kinds. Negative disruption, when my company or department was reorganized in some way and I faced the peril of losing my job or being assigned to a task that I wasn't fond of. Positive Disruption, when I seized opportunities and proposed changes or implemented new processes—things that made me feel good, that improved the companies I worked for, and that occasionally even helped my employer improve sales.

Being a positive disruptor is fun. You head to work in the morning thinking about the challenges that await you, and you finish the workday feeling good about what you accomplished.

But you need tools. You don't just go in one day and start changing things. You need a few basic skills and the courage to propose new ideas—the kind of courage you can muster when you have a solid backup plan for your personal life and both competence and confidence in your professional life.

This is a business book. Its ultimate goal is to give you the tools that you need to be a positive disruptor. Why would you want to do that? Because it's satisfying to change things for the better. Being part of change initiatives gives you something new and different to put on your résumé, something that will help you stand apart when you seek that next position. And also, because you're drawing a paycheck now, someone is paying you to work every day—shouldn't you give it your all?

Before any of us can *be* disruptors, we need strategies for dealing with the disruption that happens *to* us. A prelude to becoming an effective change agent is accepting that there are certain things that we can't control. We can cope with them by developing backup plans, figuring out what we'd do, and understanding the adjustments that can be made so that we still have a way to cover our basic needs. Then we can "park the worry," store it in the back of our brains, and forge forward.

The first two chapters of this book are about creating a safety net to roll with the punches and not let a negative career event destroy you. For me to feel comfortable as a change agent, I needed to consider my financial preparedness and my employment readiness, so I developed ways to tackle those elements. They are, effectively, a personal toolkit:

- A *financial plan* covering how I'd adjust my personal life if my job suddenly went away.
- A *skills plan* for keeping my skills current.
- A *marketing plan* for how I'd get myself known to a broader professional community, taking positive action so that new opportunities could easily find

me—and so that I'd have people to turn to if I found myself seeking new employment.

My approach was haphazard at first. For a while, the changes were hitting me so rapidly that I barely knew which end was up; I was just doing things to stay afloat. But then a pattern emerged. Certain actions helped me achieve peace of mind, helped me park the nervousness about what was out of my control. When you are no longer consumed by worry about what negative things might happen to you, you can take a breath and plunge forward enthusiastically.

The remaining chapters focus on the awareness and skills you need to develop to *become* a positive disruptor, which is the professional piece of your toolkit. Once disruption stops being your foe, it can be your friend. You can be a positive force for change. And in doing so, you can set yourself apart from the others in your industry so that you're the one chosen when the next big opportunity comes up.

Here's what my professional toolkit looks like:

- *Learning to stand apart* from the rest of the "pack," with a focus on relentless preparation: if you think you're not as smart or as quick as the others, you can compensate by being the best prepared, the most practiced.

- *Understanding myself and other people*: you can figure out how to adjust your natural behaviors to effectively approach the people from whom you need support and get them to listen to you.
- *Mastering some basic negotiation techniques*: Positive Disruption involves persuading people to stop their current routine and change their actions. When you're trying to persuade people to do something different, you're negotiating.
- *Creating Positive Disruption*: find ideas that will work, then leverage the skills in your toolkit to transform your workplace.

Of course, there are competencies you need to master that are unique to the exact position you hold. A teacher must understand his subject, a CPA must master the tax code, etc. This strategy complements that competency. This is about how you scope out the company culture, the individuals you are working with, the people whose support you need. The pieces you didn't learn in college. How you take your technical skills and put them to work.

We each can create Positive Disruption—positive change—by using the skills in our toolkits, along with the basic professional knowledge we already have, to make a favorable impact on the workplace. And that's the big payoff. We are doing something to help our current employers. We are also enhancing our own résumés, setting ourselves up so that we can clearly demonstrate how we've created transformation.

You've heard the term "win-win situation"? This is it.

GETTING ORGANIZED

May 2015, New Brunswick, New Jersey. I was invited to speak at my alma mater's Senior Send-Off, a lovely event where students, their parents, and the faculty get together to celebrate the accomplishment of finishing school and graduating with an engineering degree. That's where I started, with an engineering degree from Rutgers. Now here I was, more than four decades later, taking the stage to impart my wisdom to these hopeful graduates in their transition from college life to the working world. The corporate working world, that is, and I had plenty of thoughts to share. In the forty-plus years since my own graduation, I'd learned a lot.

Several hundred people gathered under a big tent on the lawn in front of the engineering building on that beautiful spring day. The dean was there, along with some faculty. Everyone had eaten lunch, had engaged in various activities within their respective departments, and was settling in for coffee and dessert and to listen to a few speakers. The day was winding down, and a short, impactful speech would be a perfect ending to the day's events.

I could give these future engineers the speech they expected, about how well their college education had prepared them for the workplace, or about all the grand adventures that lay ahead for them in their careers. Would those words make a difference in the lives of these students? Would a speech like that help them in their careers? Or should I present what they needed to hear?

I looked out at the sea of happy faces of all these young people who had no idea how their lives would change in the coming years. This was no time for a placating talk on hope and reflection. I had ten minutes and I wanted to make it count.

I said, "You guys are all celebrating today, and then you're going to go home. Some of you will take a few weeks off, and some of you will go to graduate school." The students smiled politely, and some of them nodded their heads in agreement.

"Most of you will be going to work in the next couple of months. Out there in the world, at the companies you're going to work for, there is some distasteful, horrible job that nobody wants to do. And right now, someone is saying, 'Hey, when is that new kid going to start?'" Chuckles wafted through the crowd.

"First of all, my advice to you is to recognize that whatever you get, whatever the new kid gets as that entry assignment, has nothing to do with the quality of the assignments and the challenges that you'll face going forward. It's just the get-your-feet-wet kind of thing that is important for learning how business operates in your firm. It helps you figure out what's what and who's who." Sighs of relief from the graduates evaporated into the warm air.

"The other thing I would tell you is that, in a year, a whole bunch of you are going to be out of work because of nothing that has anything to do with how good you are, or how smart you are, or how hard you worked. That, in fact, there is churn that takes place in corporate America. Maybe your job will be moved to a country that you don't want to move to. Maybe your company will be bought by a bigger entity that already has enough people who do what you do. There are countless things that can happen that are out of your control. You have to recognize that will happen."

I continued, "The best thing that you can do over the next couple of weeks is to think about your backup plan. How are you going to create a cushion, a 'Plan B,' so that when that inevitable day comes, and that job you thought you were going to have forever comes to an end, you won't be in a panic? You'll know what to do to help yourself through the disruption of job loss and having to find something else to do." Then, I proceeded to give them some ideas.

I hadn't noticed, but while I was speaking, a line of parents had formed alongside the podium. As I stepped away from the microphone, the dad of a new graduate approached me.

"That's the best advice my daughter could have gotten!" he stated, vigorously pumping my hand. "Thank you for telling it like it is." The next parent said the same, then the next. All these moms and dads, grandmas and grandpas, agreed on the message. "If I was going to give my child any advice right now," said a dad, "that's exactly what I'd say. Thank you."

WELCOME TO THE CHURN

Choosing that message over the traditional Senior Send-Off advice was the honest choice to make. You see, I went to work for a Fortune 50 multinational manufacturing company upon graduation from engineering school, and in the ensuing four decades, I lived through eighteen reorganizations. That doesn't mean I hit the street eighteen times, but it does mean that, eighteen times, something major happened that put me in danger of becoming jobless. Maybe my company was sold to a larger entity that already had plenty of talent in my field. Often, a reorganization made my current job go away. Sometimes, I easily got a chance to interview for a new job, but occasionally, I had to scramble. Maybe the reason was a physical relocation, a new boss, or a new corporate strategy. Some event beyond my control disrupted my life, and I had to convince someone—again—that I was the right person for another position.

Due to corporate churn, somebody would inevitably push the reset button, and everything I had—the steady job, dependable schedule, built-in corporate network, long-term career path, and regular income—would all go away. That day will come for you, and it can be paralyzing. But you can prepare for it now while you're gainfully employed. You can choose proactivity over paralysis.

At some point during those eighteen downsizes, rightsizes, reorgs, mergers, and buyouts, it became clear that job disruption was going to be a perpetual, ongoing condition of working in the corporate environment, and I needed to develop a skillset to cope with it. That skillset wasn't covered in college, of course, and it certainly wasn't included in any corporate training program. My personal method for thriving amid the constant disruption of the corporate workplace evolved. I learned how to "embrace the churn." Somewhere along the line, I started to understand that it could be a good thing, that it sometimes forces us to get out of our comfort zones and try something new.

My husband and I created backup plans for recovering from any potentially devastating effects of job loss.

(He's had some churn of his own, and occasionally, it's been simultaneous with mine.) We had to ask ourselves hard questions about how we could downsize quickly if either of us suddenly stopped working and how we would cover our essential expenses if the paychecks suddenly stopped coming.

In the beginning, when I sensed an organizational change was coming, I'd carry worry with me 24/7. It was my constant companion, a knot in my forehead at the top of my nose, just where the stuffiness is when you have a sinus infection. I'd snap at people, and I had no energy. But over time, the more we had a family plan for recovery and the better prepared I was for the next job, the less either of us worried.

A backup plan helps you create a soft landing. But then there are actions to take to catapult yourself into a whole new place. And it's different for everyone. In my case, I kept my résumé up to date and made myself known to the professional community so that if I had to look for a new job, I wouldn't be starting from ground zero. As social media came into existence, I developed a social media presence and made sure people were finding me online.

Regularly, I looked at postings for new jobs—not because I wanted to leave, but because I wanted to understand what kinds of skills employers were looking for. Keeping your knowledge and skills current helps you contribute better at your current company, and if you are mindful about your knowledge development, it will help you get the next job, too. A focus on remaining relevant will help you land softly when your company or industry encounters upheaval.

Then something unintentional happened. Once there was a fallback plan in place and I wasn't consumed by worry, I became a better employee. My skills improved, and I took prudent business risks. I wasn't afraid to try something new or look at an old problem in a new way. I was productive and had fun in the process.

Thanks to the feedback we get from our supervisors, I had a reasonable sense of my strengths and my weaknesses and was habitually examining the characteristics of the people with whom I worked so that I could pitch my ideas to them more effectively. I had to understand my preferences, learn how to adjust my actions based on the situation and the people I was dealing with, and master basic negotiating techniques to influence people to view problems and solutions from my point of view. It's about doing what is needed for a situation, which isn't always what comes naturally.

This book is about embracing the churn by acquiring tools that allow us to thrive in today's corporate world as change agents—

positive disruptors. It's about creating a cushion in case you fall back, and a way of working to help move you forward.

FILL YOUR TOOLKIT

Each person's toolkit is unique because it's influenced by many factors, including where you are in your life and your career. For example, I'm a baby boomer and an empty nester, so I have more time to dedicate to acquiring skills than a millennial who's working, is going to graduate school part-time, or has a baby on the way. And I need to focus on keeping my skills current, because those of us who have been in the workplace a long time have to guard against becoming technology dinosaurs. Someone right out of college doesn't have that problem, but they face many years of disruption ahead and need to make sure that their personal plans are in place—that their personal toolkits are growing. It takes time, but if you do a little bit each week, you'll get there.

Today, I'm grateful for all these years of corporate churn. The high demands of having to reinvent myself with every new role forced me to become effective with my skills and my knowledge, and I learned to quickly leverage everything I knew from one position to the next. What I learned in pharmaceuticals and consumer products helped me in the beverage industry, which was a springboard for financial services, global professional services, facilities management, and now, consulting. Leaving one company, a mentor told me that I had just spent "eighteen years in MBA school." He was right. We leave every job with additional knowledge and a sense of how to operate in that company's corporate culture—and if we're observant, plenty of ideas to bring to the next one.

The chapters in this book are organized like successive building blocks of knowledge that constitute the instruments you need in your toolkits. Your individual circumstances, preferences, strengths, and weaknesses determine where you need to do the most work—it's different for everyone.

Chapter One is about the corporate workplace. The churn there is real, and to thrive in it, you have to understand it and accept it.

Chapter Two focuses on taking ownership for how you are going to deal with that churn—your personal plan that will help you end up in a good place because you've been taking actions all along to prepare for inevitable negative events.

Chapter Three delves into the practice of relentless preparation. This chapter is a bridge which applies to both your personal and professional lives. Thoughtful preparation can help you stand apart from other candidates in the job market, and adopting a mindset of being prepared can help you succeed in the workplace.

Chapter Four is about you and the people around you—how you need to operate and how you might want to adjust your style and communications to be more effective in your current environment. You'll learn how understanding your preferences and tolerances—and those of the people with whom you interface—can make you more productive in your current position and more effective, quickly, in a new one.

In Chapter Five, we'll dig into negotiation, a consistently popular business topic. This is not about negotiating corporate mergers or ending trade wars. It's about getting coworkers, employers, and the people around you to do what you'd like them to do, or at least get pretty close. I'll share some examples of negotiating techniques that have served me and others well over the years. The methodical planning that goes into creating a backup plan is similar to the thinking you put in prior to negotiating something, so by the time you get to this chapter, you'll have acquired a good foundation.

Chapter Six will show you how to use the tools you've developed to create Positive Disruption that benefits yourself and your company. With the skills and perspectives gained from earlier chapters, as well as the observations you obtain by taking a hard look at the processes all around you, you can become an "agent of change," someone who embraces the churn and seeks new ideas for improvement personally and in your workplace.

Finally, Chapter Seven pulls it all together simply and concisely, so you finish reading with a reminder of how the elements build upon each other.

We live in an age when churn is inevitable. It will strike us all. You can be a victim of it, or you can practice Positive Disruption and use it to your advantage. My hope in writing this book is that you will learn from my experiences and apply my lessons to create and develop your own toolkit as a platform for doing work that you feel proud of.

KEY POINTS

- This book is organized to give you the foundation and successive building blocks for creating a toolkit of skills and practices that will help you achieve more at work in spite of the change and churn that is out of your control.

- The ultimate goal is for all of us to become positive disruptors: agents of change who set ourselves apart by embracing new ideas and transforming business, with the confidence to rebound if things don't work out the way we planned.

CHAPTER ONE

SURROUNDED BY CHURN

I came face-to-face with churn in a New Jersey machine shop. In a new position as a manufacturing manager, I was feeling pretty good about myself. One day, a machinist took me aside to show me what he had hidden in his tool cart. The older man pulled opened a drawer and pointed to a yellowed, dog-eared piece of paper he had taped to the bottom. It named every manufacturing manager he had worked for during his twenty-seven years with the company. The list was long—more than twenty-seven names—and next to each one was written the person's start and end date. *First and last name, start date, dash, end date.*

At the bottom of the list was a name with a start date, a

dash, and no end date. *Joanna Martinez*, it said. I felt like I was looking at my own tombstone. The man smiled as if to say, "You may think you're important now, but don't get too comfortable. I've outlasted all these manufacturing managers who were here before you." Indeed, according to his list, they were turning over a new manager about every ten months.

Recognizing some of the names, I called the people to see if the machinist was just making it up. No, it was real; those people all said they had worked there, but there had been a change of some sort, and they left for another assignment. *Holy Hannah*, I thought to myself, *we're not going through a disruptive period here—this is how things are and have been for years.* That was my rude awakening, but it was also my moment of enlightenment. After that day, I kept track of every time I lost a position due to something beyond my control that happened at a company. It didn't take long to realize that disruption wasn't the exception—it was the nature of the beast that had become corporate America.

IT'S NOT YOUR FAULT

"Chaos is the new normal." I heard that from Chris Sawchuk of The Hackett Group. It's truer today than ever before, and you need to accept and even embrace it, because it's not going to go away.

The fact that much of this is beyond your control is worth noting, because oftentimes, you can do everything right and still lose your job. As an example, in another assignment, I ran a small factory making dermatological products. One of them, an acne medicine, was being tested for effectiveness when a study showed some fascinating results. The medicine didn't just treat acne; it also made wrinkles disappear. Almost overnight, we had this blockbuster product on our hands. Sales skyrocketed.

Now, you would think that my career would have skyrocketed, too, but our facility was too small to handle the demand for the product. The facility was shut down, and manufacturing was moved to a bigger site. That was the right decision for the company to make, because we never would have been able to add the space, machinery, and people we needed quickly enough to capitalize on the sudden demand. But now, here I was again—a manager with nothing to manage. I had to prove to the company that I was worth keeping, and I found myself jockeying for a position at the bigger facility, starting all over with people who didn't know me.

It wasn't just bad luck. This sort of churn happens every day. It's happening right now to somebody in some shop somewhere, probably even somewhere in the company you're currently working for. Or to you.

It's not only manufacturing that's affected, either. There's churn in every industry to a certain degree. Even in the medical field, you could be a well-respected physician with a good practice when your local hospital expands its mission and decides that it wants to buy your practice. Or a new technology makes the techniques you've been successfully mastering for years obsolete.

WHAT DROVE THE CHURN, AND WHAT'S CONTINUING TO DRIVE IT?

Are you wondering how we got to this place? Think about the dramatic productivity increases we've seen in our lifetimes. Massive storage and computing power can retrieve, slice, and dice data and deliver information at lightning speed, and that enables rapid business decision-making. Thirty years ago, a company hired a team of accountants to keep the books, whereas today, technology can tell a company how much cash is on hand, what the sales numbers are, and anything else management needs to know about the facts of the business—in seconds. Think about how fast a machine using artificial intelligence can learn. Much faster than any of us.

Globalization and low-cost labor centers allow businesses to move human tasks to places where real estate, taxes, and human resources are much cheaper. Invention, innovation, and entrepreneurialism have exploded, too, with new ways of doing things and new companies to do them springing up, which affects anyone who's still doing things the "old" way. These changes benefit companies that can now operate better, faster, cheaper, and with fewer people, freeing up financial resources, which they can then use to buy up other companies or expand into new markets.

Hence, the churn.

My first big layoff was a major cut with a lot of positions being terminated. It was agonizing for the people losing their jobs and also for the management, the people who had to deliver the news. No one in the factory had done anything wrong; the reality was that competitors used better processes and had lower costs, and the end customers didn't see enough difference in products to justify the higher prices our company charged. One senior manager cried as he addressed the team, telling us that this would never happen again. He was wrong. As the competition became more relentless and cost pressures grew, the whole site was eventually shut down and is now a shopping mall. He didn't see it then, but it was the first of many adjustments that ended with the products being made in Brazil.

Once again, this isn't unique to manufacturing. Some young people I know work in digital advertising, a field that didn't exist twenty years ago. They help ensure that their clients' websites or products pop up on the first page of an online search. There's a tried and true process based on the keywords that people enter into search engines. But what if you're speaking into a device that's sitting on your night stand? The algorithms are different when you're using a chatbot, and the results are different. So even these new experts in a new field need to constantly learn more to stay even with the technology changes.

Job churn has a massive effect on your personal life. You may want to get married, buy a house, and start a family. You may want to get a nicer apartment, save for retirement, or enjoy some traveling. If your thoughts are occupied with worry about your job going away, how can you entertain the idea of investing a bunch of money in anything that requires monthly payments? How can you enjoy any new acquisition if you're always worried about your job?

IT'S NOT ALL BAD NEWS

As the final edits are made on this book, the US is at nearly full employment. Jobs go away, and new ones are popping up.

For example, one could have predicted that with the rise of mobile banking options, career opportunities in banking would be limited. And it's true that cash transactions are increasingly being handled with a technology solution. Yet banking employment is up, as more people are being employed to sell services instead of focusing on transactions. Lower-skilled jobs are diminishing, while higher-skilled positions are on the rise.

Insurance companies and businesses that process millions of forms use software robots to get the right information in the right place and to the right people, but someone needs to create and manage the robots. Companies need smart people who stay current with technology and embrace the possibilities of what new technologies bring to the workplace—people who are transformers.

There are choices with disruption. You can embrace it and thrive, fight it and probably fail, or flee and buy yourself some time. Fighting it means you'll live in misery, slugging it out with forces that are beyond your control. Fleeing the churn means delaying the inevitable. If you decide it's not for you, you can move to another industry or job with more stability and fewer disruptions. Some industries move more slowly than others, and fleeing the churn of your current workplace may make sense for a while if you find a safe place to land that fits your pace. But it's only a delay.

FIRST, ACCEPT IT

What's the takeaway? There is churn. It exists, and now is the time for you to look around and recognize it. It won't go away. You can let it scare you into career paralysis, but that won't prepare you for the next hostile takeover. There's always going to be competition. But there's also always room for someone who stands out and can adapt good practices from the industry they're working in and bring them to another.

Your choice—the best choice—is to be proactive. Adaptable. Transformative. Inertia and denial are not your friends. Action and forward thinking are what you need.

That doesn't mean you drop everything and work on the suggestions in this book until your head is ready to explode. Start small. Start with a few modest steps.

Is the world being disruptive to you? Be disruptive back.

KEY POINTS

- Churn exists, and it's not going away.

- No industry or position is immune to this churn, so throughout your working career, you'll have to adapt and adjust many times.

- Fear causes inertia. Remove the fear by having a backup plan.

QUESTIONS FOR THE READER

1. What are you worried about right now in your chosen career?

2. What changes are taking place in your company that might affect your specific position?

CHAPTER TWO

TAKE CHARGE

There was a year at work when I accomplished nothing. *Nothing.* When it came time to write up my accomplishments against my annual objectives, I realized that I'd spent the entire year being a nervous wreck. Signs of an impending reorganization had paralyzed me with fear.

At the time, I was my family's primary breadwinner and was terrified of a job loss. I'm a worrier by nature and had let worry consume my life. So instead of making things happen in my job, I rested on my laurels and good reputation—and wasted the year.

What a wake-up call. I had allowed things that were beyond my control to control me—and I didn't want to spend the next thirty years trying to duck the ax, keeping my head down so that it wouldn't get whacked. I had to take charge.

I needed to accept that this kind of change was taking place everywhere. I had to reconfigure myself to be productive in the workplace, be happy at home, and get beyond the nervousness and fear that came with all the career disruption. Fear is paralyzing, and taking action frees that mass of worry and allows you to move forward.

I could change careers and find a job in an industry that didn't experience so much churn. My other option was to change my attitude and outlook, and to *embrace the churn.*

There were tools I needed, and I set about acquiring them.

YOUR PERSONAL TOOLKIT

Your personal toolkit should include both financial and employment readiness components. In the event that you are temporarily out of work, how are you going to find that next position (or have that position find you), and how will you pay the bills in the interim? Everyone's in a different situation, so everyone's plan will look a little different. But as mentioned in the introduction, you should ponder these three areas:

· A *financial plan*, in case your current employment situation changes abruptly
· A *skills plan* for how you'll keep your skills current,

which improves your readiness for the next opportunity

- A way to make yourself known—effectively, a *marketing plan*

Mark Twain said, "I've lived through some terrible things in my life, some of which actually happened." His point was that we worry too much. But for some of us, thinking through the worst-case scenario and developing a plan for how to deal with it is a way to quash that worry. Ask yourself, "What's the worst that can happen in my career, and how would I deal with it?" As you think about what action you'd take, any paralysis or preoccupation that's gripping you will diminish. The best way to deal with those worst-case, hopefully-never-gonna-happen scenarios is to plan for them. Then, park them and move on.

A FINANCIAL SAFETY NET

One of the best things that ever happened to me was the opportunity to work in a financial services company. Surrounded by screens showing stock market performance and the latest financial news, it was impossible for employees not to become aware of the value of keeping their personal finances organized. You may not have the kind of portfolio that big investors have, but you need to know what you have and where it is. Even if you have nothing more than a spreadsheet that you update once or twice a year, getting your financial information pulled together is a massive step forward.

In the early years when you're new to the workplace, it might be a challenge to save very much. Maybe you are barely making ends meet. Then you just have to think through what your safety net might look like. Maybe you can't put more in the bank, so maybe it won't be about improving your assets—maybe it will be more about reducing your expenses if you need to.

Look at your current expenses, and evaluate how restrictive they are with regard to your overall financial status. How can you adjust if you have to make changes quickly? How do you earn more if you need to, or spend less? If you just moved out of your parents' home, maybe you ask them to leave your bedroom open for a while, instead of turning it into a Pilates studio too quickly. That way, you can move back in temporarily if you have to. Maybe you can add roommates if you ever need to or rent out space via Airbnb. Before you sign up for any service that comes with a monthly payment, read the contract. Is it something you can get out of easily, or are you going to be locked into a large payment plan every month for a year or longer? Think and reevaluate before you sign.

However modest, there *can* be a plan if you put in the effort.

Break the mindset of immediate satisfaction, and create a new mindset that focuses less on the short term and more on long-term peace of mind. Think twice about buying that nifty little sports car. Instead, drive a car that's slightly below your income standard, and then invest the money you would have spent on that big car payment. Delay that elaborate vacation; Machu Picchu isn't going anywhere.

There are countless ways to adopt a goal-oriented savings plan, and the sum of little things can be substantial. The benefits of shifting your mindset are twofold. You're building savings for your worst-case scenario, and you're also learning how to decrease your expenses to the bare minimum, in case you're out of work and your income suddenly stops.

Keep in mind that while job churn can put you out of work temporarily, you may also get to a point in your career when you want to *put yourself* out of work, to do something different. Developing a plan to create "walking out the door money" allows you to be in charge, regardless of the situation.

A SKILLS PLAN FOR EMPLOYMENT READINESS

One of my favorite bosses suffered from "encore anxiety." No matter how much he succeeded or how many big deals he did, he was consumed by worry that he'd never be able to repeat his success. Have you ever felt like that? Have you ever wondered if you'll ever find a job as good as the one you have now?

To deal with that, another part of your personal toolkit is the creation and ongoing development of an employment readiness plan. Industries change rapidly, and you need to be constantly assessing what employers are looking for—and making sure you acquire or update those skills.

FIND YOUR "SPARK"

The travel industry has been affected by a lot of automation and consolidation, and as a result, there are many displaced travel people out there with good, solid experience. We were once in search of someone to lead a travel program, so as most companies do, the position was posted online. Because of the churn in the travel industry, we received an immediate response—nearly 400 résumés popped up overnight, posted by people hoping to fill the role.

But they all looked the same. Every applicant had similar, cookie-cutter accomplishments and certifications. How do you choose candidates to interview when everyone looks the same? Do you choose the person living closest to the office? Do you line up the applications and use a random number generator to choose who will come in? What process can you put in place that's fair? To an employer trying to operate ethically, it's a real issue.

Even if you're employed right now, think of yourself as a potential candidate for your next position. What is the point of difference between you and others in your field? What kind of accomplishments set you apart, so that you are the person chosen for an interview?

You need to stand out. You need to find your Spark, the quality or accomplishment or characteristic that differentiates you from the people against whom you are competing.

For many years, I met new people every week, usually potential suppliers who wanted to sell to the company I worked for. When asked what set them apart from their competitors, the most frequent response was "Our team has (thirty, sixty, 120, etc.) years of experience among us." We'd sit in meeting after meeting where that was the response. But "years of experience" isn't a point of difference. In some industries, such as technology, it can be a detriment, as companies look for partners with the latest and greatest product "born in the cloud," not something that's twenty years old and has been modified over and over.

Start thinking about your Spark right now. I'll tell you more about what you can do to differentiate yourself and stand out in Chapter Three, "Stand Apart," and in Chapter Six, "Ready, Set, Go." What is unique about *you*?

CONSTANTLY BUILD YOUR SKILLSET

You need to be in a state of almost constant market assessment. Think beyond the job you have now, and look at the marketplace. Your employer's tools and processes may not be as current as the industry leaders, and even if they're in sync now, they may not be in the future. That's why you have to examine trends and see what employers are looking for in a new hire. You can read industry journals, review job boards, or talk to a recruiter to find out which skills are valued in your field, and then do an honest appraisal of your own capabilities and see how you stack up. Understand the hot, new trends; then, get yourself the knowledge or experience they require.

Personally, every two years, I took a deep look at what was being asked for in the positions to which I aspired. For a while, the emphasis on *quality* was new. The company I was with was undergoing a quality-improvement endeavor, and I volunteered to be a quality trainer. It meant a lot more work for a few months, but I learned the concepts, taught the classes, and suddenly had another sought-after bullet to put on my résumé.

International experience or at least evidence of a world

mindset is important now. The workplace operates more globally now than when I started, and many of you are working for multinational companies. Communication, decision-making, and the whole process of running a company differ across borders. For many people, cross-cultural understanding can be a very useful tool. Volunteer for that assignment to work with folks outside the US, and remember not to assume that your way of working is the right way to get things done.

If you think getting a particular skill is out of reach for one reason or another, do some research. You might be surprised by what you discover. My friend Janice never finished college. Her lack of a degree kept coming up in job interviews, and she wanted to do something about it, but she knew that college was expensive and she just didn't have the funds. Recently, in her late forties, she went back to school and found that cost wasn't the impediment she thought it would be. The school she selected considered older students part of their diversity population, and she received more funding than she had ever expected.

Frequently, companies subsidize education, so if there's further training or certification offered, take it. You don't necessarily have to commit to another college degree. Many certifications can be earned in a matter of days or weeks, and most courses are offered virtually, so you can get certified in a new skill from your computer.

In the end, the point is that all of us should be aware of the latest advances in our field or industry and get some practical experience if possible. When it's not, then some basic training or enough knowledge to be able to hold a decent conversation on the topic are the next best things—anything to help stand out from the pack.

YOUR PERSONAL MARKETING PLAN

You've probably heard a million times that—in addition to finding good opportunities—you have to make it easy for good opportunities to find you. This means developing a network of professionals and otherwise making yourself known so that people will think of you when a good opportunity arises.

At the start of my career, social media didn't exist. But it still made sense to take positive action to get my name out. Heck, I once got a call for a great position by a headhunter who saw a response I gave to a Q&A column in a professional publication—just two paragraphs, which took just a few minutes to write.

Today, it's necessary to have a positive social media presence. Whether or not you take the initiative to create and manage an online presence, information on you is already all over the web, and the image portrayed may not be the one you want employers to see. No matter how you find a new position or apply for it, *someone* along the line *somewhere* is going to do an online search to see how you pop up. You need an intentional plan for presenting yourself online regularly and in the way you want to be presented. It's almost guaranteed that recruiters and potential employers will check out potential candidates online. What will they find if they look for you?

About a dozen years ago, my good friend Emily and I were testing out our names in search engines. We plugged her name in, and the screen immediately painted an accurate picture of her life. She was a teacher, and there was a newspaper article about an Earth Day project she had done with her students. She was on the board of an organization that helped the disabled, and there was an announcement about a fundraiser. We found her mentioned in the minutes of the local garden club and in the local newspaper when a student she had mentored won an award. The search results went on and on, painting a rich and accurate picture of Emily's full life.

We were interrupted, and it wasn't until much later that I sat down and plugged my own name in. What did I see? A bunch of raunchy photos appeared of someone with the same name as mine, along with a link to her Facebook page. I had to scroll a bit before *this* Joanna Martinez's photo showed up. I was stunned.

Emily had an outstanding online profile by virtue of the activities she was involved in, and she was pleasantly surprised by the extent of her positive social media presence. I was actively working at it—or so I thought—and was nearly invisible. How could I increase my presence so that someone looking for me online would actually find *me* and not someone twenty years younger in a vastly different profession? The women whose name I shared had obviously done a better job of figuring out how to use the internet to their advantage than I had.

What I needed to do, and what you need to do, is have enough mentions captured online that when your name goes into a search engine, the real you pops up among the others, at or near the top of the list. You can't make the others go away, but you can try to make sure you're the first one people will see.

So without paying someone for help, how do you get your name and qualifications to pop up? You can comment on a LinkedIn article, for example, volunteer to appear on a discussion panel, or give a presentation to get your name out there in a positive light and help establish yourself as an expert—or at least someone "in the know"—in your industry. There are many other ways to do this with personal and professional networking sites, blogs, photos, and involvement in industry or personal events that reflect who you are and what you want a potential employer to see. In general, the more active you are online, by providing your own content or being featured in someone else's content, the more likely you'll show up in a search. Make that content and those interactions count.

Since that search engine experience, I've made a habit of posting more regularly. But even today, after many years of speaking, publishing articles, and so on, I still struggle to be on the first page of a Google search. With a reasonably common name it will always be a challenge, I suppose. There are a lot of Joanna Martinezes out there. Guaranteed, all of you with common names like mine will find plenty of companions on the page when you type in your name. Make a habit of doing a search regularly. You might be surprised by what you find.

There are plenty of ways to bomb on social media, too, and lots of examples out there of celebrities, politicians, and everyday business professionals who have done serious damage to their brands by not understanding how to use it to their advantage instead of their detriment. Think consciously about presenting yourself in the way that you want to be presented. If you want to be the rugby-playing frat boy, go ahead; but understand that image of you might someday affect your ability to be taken seriously in the engineering job that you want. (The particular nephew I am talking about here knows who he is. Remember, Aunt Jo is watching.)

Anyone who attends a professional conference can volunteer to speak or participate in a panel discussion. Many conferences will cover the transportation and room costs for their presenters, so it may be a way for you to get out there and network even if you are working in a company where there are no extra funds for training or personal development. By virtue of your participation, you get mentioned in the publicity and brochures that the organization publishes; it's a way to multiply the places where your name shows up in a positive way in an online search.

So there you have it: some of the things you can set in motion to organize the personal side of your life. The elements in this chapter describe what worried me personally and also explain the actions that I took. Your worries, weaknesses, and plans may be different. Doesn't matter—just confront the things that worry you as a result of business churn and ponder how to harness them. And move on to populating your professional toolkit.

KEY POINTS

- At a minimum, your personal toolkit should contain three elements:

  - A *financial plan* for the days when unwanted disruption occurs

  - A *skills plan* to improve your readiness for that next assignment

  - A personal *marketing plan* for making yourself known in your field, with a strong online presence so you can be found when you want to be found—become, effectively, a virtual employment seeker.

- There is plenty of competition out there. You need to be able to clearly articulate what sets you apart from others against whom you may be competing—your Spark.

QUESTIONS FOR THE READER

1. How can you make your financial situation more flexible so that you can easily downshift if you need to? What can you do today to start developing a financial cushion to get you through the next career disruption?

2. What can you do to develop a new skill that will make it easier for you to get another job?

3. What are you doing, and what else can you do, to improve your online presence and make it easier for recruiters and hiring managers to find you?

4. What's your *Spark*?

CHAPTER THREE

STAND APART

One of my favorite visuals is a sketch of a sea of fish. Most are blue; one is gold. This book in many ways is about making yourself into the gold one—the one who gets noticed.

If you're following the suggestions from the first two chapters, you're already taking steps to distinguish yourself with an online presence that will help you expand your network and have good opportunities come to you. As you start to look at enhancing your professional skills, there are actions you can take that will distinguish your approach from others, and bold moves that will help you contribute to your company in new, better ways—more ways to help find that Spark from Chapter Two.

RELENTLESS PREPARATION

Have you ever watched someone take command of a discussion or a situation at work or at home? There is always someone who appears smarter, faster, or more eloquent than you perceive yourself to be—or so you think. Maybe they're just better prepared. Perhaps they've read the meeting documents ahead of time. Or they have pondered the likely questions and are ready with answers.

As a finalist for a coveted position at a well-regarded firm, I knew that my primary competitor had a wonderful résumé that was very similar to mine, except that he had experience with companies that were bigger, better known, and more prestigious. I still managed to make my way through successive rounds of interviews, but I knew that I was at a disadvantage—at least on paper. Within days of my final interview, I happened to be at a networking event and mentioned the interview to someone. That person's response changed my entire strategy.

"You obviously want this job," the person said, "but what have you done to set yourself apart from your competition?"

My immediate response was to list my obvious attributes: brains, accomplishments, work ethic, personality, etc. Her comeback was, "None of the things you just said are big enough reasons to give you the job over someone else, especially if this person has the blue-chip résumé you say he has."

Just what you need, right? Someone giving you another task. I really didn't want to do anything extra. It was summer, and even though I really wanted that position, I had the lethargy that sets in when it's hot outside and all you want to do is float in the pool. But I called a few trusted advisors, and they all agreed with her.

As I noodled on it a bit, an idea popped up. I created a one-page chart—basically a bunch of boxes drawn on a page—outlining the company's issues that had come up in previous interviews, and then I added what I believed were some good solutions based on my experience. In areas where I had no experience, I called people in my network to get their advice. It chewed up a day, but I was fairly certain my opponent wouldn't take that extra step. After all, if he had done his homework as I had, he probably knew that his résumé was "bigger" than mine.

The final interview was scheduled for midafternoon on a swelteringly hot day in July. The gentleman interviewing me was stuck in a meeting and was running late. I waited nervously, clutching a portfolio of my credentials and sweating to death in my business clothes. The midsummer sun beat down through the huge, plate-glass windows of that high-rise building, and it seemed like I sat there forever. The executive finally appeared, greeted me warmly, and sat down behind his desk. Then, he closed his eyes. He didn't ask me any questions at all. He simply closed his eyes, leaned back in his chair, and sat there. *Was it a test? Was it some sort of psychological trick to see how I would handle myself?*

At first, I didn't know what to do. There was a moment of silence while I waited for his first question, a question that didn't come. Then, I remembered my chart. I took it out of my portfolio, held it up, and started to talk.

"I learned about some challenges you're having in the company, and you might be interested to know how I would handle things if I were hired for this position. So, I prepared this," I said. There was no reaction. He just sat there with his eyes closed. *Was he awake or had he dozed off?* I started talking again. "Here's how other companies are handling similar problems, and here's how I would tackle them in my first few weeks on the job." I stepped him through each issue and what I would do to solve it. I even asked myself questions like "How much would that cost?" and "That sounds good, but what if we did this instead?" And then I answered them. I continued on like that for about twenty minutes.

The gentleman finally opened his eyes. Later, I learned that he was a hard-working, wonderful executive who began his day very early and would understandably be a little tired by late afternoon. To this day, I don't know what he heard or didn't hear, whether he closed his eyes on purpose or not. (It's one of those questions you just don't ask.) But the fact that I was unusually well prepared saved me from becoming rattled. I made up for the fact that I didn't have the top résumé by preparing something for that interview that no one else had prepared. It showed him that I was paying attention to the company's challenges. It positioned me as a problem-solver and showed I was willing to put the time and effort into helping him out before I was even hired.

If I hadn't prepared that chart, what would I have done while he sat there with his eyes closed? I could have talked about myself, which is what most people do during an interview. Instead, I talked about his business and his challenges. Being prepared saved the day. And I got the job.

Later on, I heard a different executive say that I was chosen because I was so well prepared. It's a lesson that I'll never forget.

You're probably never going to be in a situation where your interviewer closes his eyes, but you *will* be in situations where you have to set yourself apart. Making an effort that no one else is willing to make, or taking a risk that no one else is willing to take, are examples of how you take the first step to becoming the lone goldfish in a very large ocean.

Being prepared can make up for a lot of shortcomings or gaps in your natural skillset, too. During a class on negotiation, I mentioned that I wasn't the best natural negotiator. One of the students called me out on that. "Why did I pay for this course if I'm not learning from the best?" he asked. That student had missed a key point. You don't have to be the best negotiator, and you don't have to be the fastest person when thinking on your feet. But you *do* need to be aware of your weaknesses and put in the time and effort necessary to become well prepared. Thorough preparation compensates for the gaps in anyone's natural style. Not everyone is born to be a master negotiator or the life of the party, and not everyone thinks quickly on their feet—but if you recognize your weaknesses, you can go a long way by putting in the time to be well prepared.

GET BACK ON THAT BIKE

Remember learning how to ride a bike? You went up and down the driveway, over and over again. You practiced until you got it right and accepted that you would get bruised and scraped along the way.

Why aren't you doing that at work? Why aren't you running through the points you want to make before the meeting starts, so you can come across as professional and get people to pay attention to you?

We've already mentioned participation in conferences as a way to get yourself more widely known. Public speaking is easy if you are outgoing but can be really hard if you are shy. I was such a nervous speaker that more than once, I vomited after talking (thankfully, never onstage).

A friend in Canada had a similar obstacle, and we started trading tips on how to be more at ease when expressing opinions and standing in front of people. There was a ton of material out there to help us and many people to ask for advice. From neck massages to rotating our shoulders to shaking our hands and legs before going onstage, lots of techniques helped us make small changes. But in the end, preparation was the best antidote. *Relentless preparation.* Reviewing the points in our heads as we commuted to work, and doing dry runs with our spouses until we knew the material so well that the nervousness diminished. It wasn't so much getting out of our comfort zones as changing them. Trying again and again, even after flubbing badly. Trying until we found the right formula. Getting back on the bike after falling off.

WHO'S DONE THEIR HOMEWORK?

I once read an article about a top-producing salesman.

When asked about the secret to his success, he said that at the end of each workday, while everyone was walking out the door, he made one more call, sent one more email, or followed up on one more open item. He put forth that little bit of extra effort, and it added up over time.

Think about this. If you've prepared for a meeting and you're going into a room full of executives who are busy with one hundred other things or have become so complacent that they work off-the-cuff, you might have a piece of information, a strategy, or a way of attacking a problem that they haven't considered. It happens all the time.

You can actually walk into a meeting, look around the room, and see by body language who is prepared and who isn't. Hint: the ones who are furiously scanning the documents and avoiding eye contact are unprepared. It's similar if you're on a conference call—you can hear the hesitation in people's voices as they quickly eyeball the documents they should have read yesterday. Leadership naturally flows to the ones who are prepared; the others are too busy trying to fake it. They are spending their energy on catching up instead of moving things forward.

During my last twenty-five years working in corporations, I met at least two new people a week. That adds up to one hundred new people per year, 2,500 over the course of a quarter-century. And that's a very conservative number.

Yet most of them all mush together in my memory. Only a few stand out. Why? Because they took the time to understand our business and really learn what we needed, and then they worked hard to break the paradigms within their own companies to get it for us.

In that field of 2,500, about a dozen people come to mind. That's less than half a percent. Here are three that I will always remember:

Steve Margolis delivered extraordinary customer service. I didn't like him at first; he was "larger than life," and his strong personality took over a room when he walked in. Sometimes, I'd hear his voice booming down the hallway and say, "He's here again. Please keep him away from me." Then one day, I realized he was consistently the only person who did what he said he was going to do. We'd sit in a meeting, and everyone would have some task they agreed to handle afterward. He was the lone person who followed through. Time after time, when he said he was going to take something on, he did it.

Of course, Steve's job was to sell. But he invested the time to understand our company's problems and objectives, looked for innovations that would help us, and brought forward specific ideas. He didn't try to sell us everything in his company's portfolio; he targeted only what we needed.

Ten years later, in a different situation, Jeff Wallack took responsibility for managing a key relationship. We started poorly. In fact, the day he came in to introduce himself, I was planning to terminate our contract with his firm. More soft-spoken than Steve, he listened and demonstrated an equally strong and reliable follow-through on his commitments. This time, I was smart enough to recognize brilliant customer service when I saw it. He learned our business, eventually set sales records, and at last count, he's been promoted three times since we worked together.

Do you work for a company where people say they'll do things all the time, then don't? Sometimes, it's just part of the culture. Shockingly, something like actually delivering on your commitments may be most of what you need to do to excel. Think about how simple that is—and how few people actually do it.

David Bush is cofounder of a technology company who altered his firm's licensing agreement to meet our needs as his client. He recognized that my company's requirements were different from those of his typical client, and he adapted his licensing so that we could use his software the way we needed to. He didn't try to make us buy what he had; he did the research to know that a little tweaking was required to make our two companies harmonize.

Each of these individuals took time to understand how our company worked, where it was headed, and the challenges we faced. They came to meetings armed with ideas, and they met their commitments. They did their homework. Being prepared made a difference.

THE YODA BOOK

Today, many firms use customer relationship management software to keep track of interactions with their clients. Long before there was a technology solution, one of my mentors created what he called his *Yoda Book*. Just like the Grand Master Jedi, the book was a fount of workplace wisdom. He taught his team to record the interactions we had with internal leadership, suppliers, and external clients—anyone who was a decision maker or an important partner. The collected information helped us be better prepared, and it helped us sell our ideas within the company as well. The knowledge in the *Yoda Book* included anything that could facilitate a later conversation, anything we needed to follow up on, or any little snippets of information about competitors that might have come our way. Reviewing this information before a call helped all of us establish the quick rapport needed to work efficiently, and it also provided anyone new with a quick history of each business relationship. It was a great database, built one interaction at a time.

QUESTION YOUR OWN WORK SO SOMEONE ELSE DOESN'T HAVE TO

Early in my career, I conducted an analysis and put some calculations together for an engineering issue. My boss looked at my numbers and said, "This doesn't make sense." He was right; I had made errors. He taught me that after finishing any task, I should take a moment, step back, and ask, "Does this make sense?" If it didn't, then it needed to be reworked or at least bounced off knowledgeable colleagues. In this era of tight deadlines and heavy workloads, it's so easy to produce work filled with mistakes. There's also a tendency to trust information because it just looks so professional when it's on a beautifully organized spreadsheet. How many times have you rushed to meet a deadline and been so happy to be done that you simply handed your part of a project to someone else without double-checking your work? Resolve to stop doing that. Instead, take a deep breath, think about the problem you're trying to solve, and ask yourself (or someone else), "Does this result make sense?"

SMALL TALK

Lest I beat this topic to death, there is one more story about preparation that bears telling.

Are you always the life of the party? If so, you can skip the rest of these paragraphs. That person is never me; I always get tongue-tied when meeting new people. But there is a method to help those of us who get nervous and who are lousy at small talk. It came from an article in a teen magazine published in the 1970s. This article suggested coming up with five things to talk about before going on a date. These five topics or interesting facts should be broad enough so that other people will likely be interested in talking about them, too.

It holds true whether you're dating or heading off to a business conference. It is as simple as picking up your phone and getting something interesting off a news feed. Or making a note of that funny story you heard yesterday so you don't forget it. Or maybe it's remembering a few questions that can be conversation starters with strangers. Keep replenishing with little tidbits, and it'll be much easier the next time you're faced with a group of people you don't know. Instead of mindlessly flipping through your phone while you wait for the train, flip with a purpose.

Practice helps. A friend who liked to throw parties had a very eclectic group of acquaintances with a wide array of education, backgrounds, political and religious views, hobbies, and interests. Attending those parties gave me the chance to "work the crowd" and practice my conversational skills. It was the perfect learning environment because, unlike the workplace, if I didn't succeed, I could just go home. There's nothing like practicing on people you are likely never to see again.

Make preparation a habit. Over time, you'll do it without even thinking about it.

QUESTIONS FOR THE READER

1. What kind of preparation can you be doing to get better results and stand apart from the crowd?

2. What five things can you talk about the next time you are catapulted into a room full of strangers? If none come to mind, how will you develop a list?

CHAPTER FOUR

DO WHAT IS NECESSARY, NOT WHAT COMES NATURALLY

Have you ever noticed what it's like to work in a room that's either too warm or too cold? Or in a place where your cell phone keeps cutting out? Or where someone is breathing down your neck to meet a deadline?

All of us work more effectively and more happily when we are comfortable, when distractions are minimized and we can concentrate on the task at hand. Beyond making sure that the physical environment is right, you can increase your comfort and that of those you work with by understanding the corporate culture and the personalities you are working with, and then adapting so that your actions fit the situation. You're sending out ideas, requests, and information. This is about making sure they are received in the manner you intend. Everyone's unique personality, behaviors, strengths, weaknesses, and preferences affect how they operate in the workplace. Your strongest attributes may not be a good match with the personal characteristics of those you hope to influence, including the people you need to work with every day. So it's smart to look around and scope out the characteristics of your coworkers and those at your firm whom you hope to influence. If you understand yourself and observe the actions of the people you deal with, you can adjust how to approach them so that you do so in a way that increases their comfort and increases the chances you'll be listened to.

The better you understand your own "operational mode," the easier it will be for you to determine when to use it to your full advantage and when to tweak it to fit in, to be more readily accepted and to be more effective. You're not being disingenuous; you understand that you and someone else may have two different styles, and you are adapting your approach to be more in sync with each other. In other words, *you are removing an unnecessary distraction*.

Think about yourself. If you are a gregarious people person and are suddenly working with someone who is serious, quiet, and all business, how does that make you feel?

Do you tense up? What if you are slow and deliberate, and your coworker seems to absorb information much more quickly?

Perhaps the differences in your styles make you—or both of you—uncomfortable. But none of us can count on someone else to make changes. *You* need to take the initiative, because *you* are the one trying to be more effective.

Doesn't it make sense to scope out the people you are dealing with, such as your boss, your internal clients, and your teammates? The more you approach them in a manner that is comfortable to them, the more they will be willing to listen to you. If you understand your own style, think a little about the folks with whom you interact, and are willing to make a few adjustments, you can be more effective.

IT'S NOT ABOUT YOU; IT'S ABOUT THEM

Over coffee one morning in NYC, I was networking with the COO of a Japanese financial services institution. He nervously watched my hand gestures while I spoke, and I could see the discomfort on his face. Noticing that he sat with his hands quietly in his lap, I read the cue and put my hands on my lap as well, slowing my speech and toning down the emphasis. The change in his demeanor was instant; his face softened and relaxed. By matching my gestures and speech to his, the distraction was eliminated, and he started listening and participating in the conversation.

You've been adapting all your life, probably without really thinking about it. Do you remember the mean girls in high school? The ones who made fun of your clothes and threw food at you in the cafeteria? You found a way to deal with them. It's likely they didn't change anything themselves. But maybe you modified your behaviors and became fast friends with some of them. Maybe you found friends of your own with whom you had more in common. Whatever happened, you either adjusted your own behaviors or found a different situation where you were a better fit.

KNOW YOURSELF: HOW YOU WORK, AND HOW YOU MIGHT ADJUST

Understanding yourself and your optimal operational mode demands some introspection. Perhaps you've taken a "personality test" somewhere along the line. There are many different types of tests available that you can take online, or you can work with a professional service to take an assessment to articulate your own preferences, your natural style.

Think about the times when you were happiest and most productive at work. What were you doing, and how were you doing it? Were you working alone or with coworkers? How were you communicating—by phone, email, Skype, or face-to-face? Were you following someone's instructions, or were you in charge? Were you focused on one piece of a project or juggling multiple activities—or even multiple projects? Where do you really shine?

You'll enjoy your work more and be more effective if you put yourself in situations where you're likely to be naturally successful. For example, if you're a very creative individual who's all over the place with great ideas, then acknowledge that. Maybe you like the *idea* of being a team leader but are more suited to the creative opportunities that come with another role, while a different type of person is more ideally suited to leading. Likewise, if you're a "born leader," then working directly under a strong boss may not work for you.

Do you enjoy a dynamic environment where decisions are made quickly and you have the ability to effect change throughout your department? Or are you more comfortable in a company with a distinct chain of command, where everyone knows their place and stays in their lane? Do you prefer working as a sole contributor rather than as a member of a team? What about a culture that relies heavily on email and conference calls versus one that has an open-door policy and a lot of face-to-face communication? Those are questions only you can answer, and your responses will give you clues to the situations in which you'll naturally be the most productive.

Although you may end up in the perfect role at the perfect company for your style, you may still have to perform differently than you're used to because of circumstances outside your control. That's where your ability to adapt can pay huge dividends. Are you a naturally gregarious "road warrior" who's used to traveling for work? How are you going to do that in a company where the business-travel dollars are shrinking? If you're still expected to work with people across sites, are you comfortable with other modes of communication, like Skype? Being open to learning new ways to accomplish your goals will help you adapt more quickly to ongoing churn in the work-place environment.

Personally, I'm a parallel thinker, easily distracted, and more productive when I have many things to do. A single task will never be completed, but a long list gets accomplished because when my attention wanes, I can shift to the next item on the list, making progress in small steps on each one. Because my attention is easily diverted, I configure each task in a way that allows me to accomplish it. If I have a long presentation to prepare, I'll set small goals and allow myself a break or a reward when each one is completed. Taking that big task and breaking it down into smaller components that are easier to handle helps me adapt my personal style to projects that may not be a "natural fit."

What's comfortable for *you*? Be honest with yourself, and consider what comes most naturally to you in the workplace. What are your strengths, your weaknesses, and your preferences? How can you reconfigure the way you work to fit the task at hand?

As Kelly Barner, the career-procurement and supply-chain expert behind Buyers Meeting Point, wrote:

> I have a natural desire to take complex, undefined categories and boil them down to their core requirements and cost drivers. I prefer to consider data carefully before taking action or speaking with suppliers and stakeholders, which reduces risk even if it does present a challenge when I am thrown a curveball...[Technology] solutions provide a welcome distance between me and the supplier representatives that would park themselves in my office until an award was made if given the opportunity...

The ability to accurately read an individual or the changing dynamics of a team gives me an advantage by allowing me to react before a problem occurs. I've relied on this within project teams as well as at the program management level, watching for the reactions of executive team members in response to new processes or sourcing results.

Some of the greatest benefits to understanding my type are that I can plan around my less productive tendencies. For example:

I would prefer to avoid the telephone at all costs; therefore, I have a two-email maximum when dealing with complex or contentious issues. After that, I force myself to pick up the phone or schedule a meeting.

I am driven to complete projects on schedule, which might cost me the opportunity to vary from the schedule in return for improved results. To prevent missed opportunities, I stop at predetermined points in each project to gain objective feedback from colleagues.[1]

Kelly is doing exactly what this chapter suggests. She has a keen knowledge of herself and of the tasks at hand, and she makes the adjustments she needs to make to achieve her goals.

KNOW YOUR TOLERANCE LEVELS

While you're identifying your preferences, consider your tolerance levels as well. Knowing what you're willing to put up with—and what are deal-breakers for you in a

---

1   Kelly Barner, "Myers-Briggs for Procurement, Part 6: Personality Type in Practice," *eSourcing Forum*, Oct. 2, 2013, accessed Nov. 7, 2017, http://www.esourcingforum.com/archives/2013/10/02/myers-briggs-for-procurement-part-6-personality-type-in-practice.

working environment—will help you choose the right work situation. Personally, my tolerance for bureaucracy is low. At one point, the culture at an employer favored long, consensus-building meetings, with accompanying slides, analysis, and prework. At the end of one cold January, I realized that I had spent only ten hours that month actually moving the business forward; the rest was preparing for and sitting in long meetings that dragged on for days. I moved to a smaller, firm with a flatter organizational structure and a culture that embraced action. It was a much better match.

Whether you can tolerate bureaucracy or not—and whether you're focused or distracted, an introvert or extrovert, a lone wolf or a team player, fact-based or governed by gut feel—by understanding yourself, you can make the adjustments you need to make when the task at hand calls for actions that you might not normally take.

KNOW WHAT YOU'RE DEALING WITH: THE CORPORATE ENVIRONMENT

Once you understand your preferences and tolerance levels, you should look around and scope out the styles of the people you're dealing with. People react better and are more open when they are approached in a way that makes them comfortable. Your natural style may be the total opposite of theirs. When that's the case, if you behave as you normally would, they may very well not be as open to you and your ideas or your accomplishments as you want them to be.

When working at a European company, I became friends with a colleague who was well respected. People always paid attention to his ideas and observations. I started to watch how he did things—really paying attention to how he worked. Whenever we left a meeting, he would have five or six pages filled with notes, while I left those meetings with just a few bullet points. He would write a "white paper" with lots of details and publish it to the key stakeholders; I would put those bullet points in an email. His work style was a much better match to that of the company decision makers than mine was. He understood the corporate culture, the "ways of working" with the people at headquarters. By watching what he did and following similar methods of communication, those of us outside of the head office could be more effective. I did what came naturally to me; he did what was necessary given the culture at headquarters. People listened to him. He won.

Knowing yourself and the people you're dealing with—and having a good understanding of the larger, corporate environment—can yield great results. You just have to observe and then be willing to make some changes to your own behaviors.

KNOW WHO YOU'RE DEALING WITH: THE CHARACTERS AROUND YOU

There are lots of personality types; just look at your family and your friends. You are probably comfortable with some and perhaps clash with others. Could part of that be due to likenesses or dissimilarities in your styles?

The same thing happens at work. Below are descriptions of four individuals you may meet, with suggestions on how to adapt your behavior to effectively communicate with each one of them.

THE DRIVEN LEADER

The driven leader is the "alpha figure" in the room, a take-charge person. She is all about the results. Her calendar is packed, and she "owns the room" in every meeting she attends. She often finds fault with something right at the beginning: the agenda, the words being used, whatever. It's all about making it clear who's top dog.

She won't waste your time and doesn't want her own to be wasted, either, particularly if you are not a customer or an executive. She feels no obligation to listen to anyone who isn't central to getting a job done.

She'll be more receptive to you if you deal directly and without a lot of small talk. Approach her with the big-picture issue or solution, no drama. Have the details as a backup, but get right to the summary. In order to be heard, you need to make her understand why there is value in your request or idea. Adapt your style to her time limitations and her interests.

And make it quick. She has work to do.

THE NUMBERS PERSON

Then there's the numbers person, perhaps the chief financial officer (CFO) or head of sales. His day is filled with numbers, and his success or failure depends on how good they are: sales, profits, growth, and so on.

He will ask pointed questions and expect detailed answers. He'll arrive to meetings prepared. If you send him an email or provide him with a spreadsheet or document before you speak with him, he will almost always read it. He'll skip the words and go right to the bottom line.

Like the hard-charging leader in our first example, he has no interest in small talk, but he loves a good analysis. If you have a well-thought-out request supported by facts and figures, he will be more likely to listen to you. Do not rely on the intangible value of your ideas when dealing with a numbers person. Requests must be supported by facts and analysis. Even if he disagrees with the analysis, he will appreciate the fact that it's been thoroughly done.

He will look for "holes" in your work—make sure there aren't any.

THE PEOPLE PERSON

Next is the people person, who is very relationship-driven. These executives rely on the power of their contacts to get things done, so they forge great relationships for themselves within and outside of the company. If they believe in your idea, they'll use those connections to move it forward. They consider the "people impact" of business to be more important than do other executives. They'll greet you warmly and will be interested—or at least act interested—in what you have to say.

Adjust your style accordingly. Don't lead with a "numbers, facts, and figures" discussion, but rather, take some time to establish a friendly rapport—and then help them visualize the benefits of your plan or your request. Emphasizing other situations where this idea has been successful or having endorsements from other people can go a long way toward gaining the support of this type of person.

THE EARLY ADOPTER

The early adopter is the person with the latest high-tech gadgets. "Tech-forward" is a great description. Maybe she is the head of technology; maybe he is a millennial who's risen quickly to the executive ranks. Technology is an integral part of this person's life. They use a device for everything and try any app they can get their hands on that might make their life easier.

You're going to have to step up your technology game if you are having frequent interactions with this person. No walking over to their workspace with a sheaf of papers held together by one of those massive clips that hurts your fingers if they get caught in it. You may be used to using email; they might be posting on Slack all day. If you're using a piece of technology in front of this person, make sure you've tested it and understand how it works. If the best technology story you can think of is the day that the first PC was installed in the office, you have a lot of work ahead of you.

If you are perceived as a technology dinosaur, you will have difficulty getting this person's attention.

This is a mistake I've made myself. While juggling multiple clients who each preferred different software tools, I found myself often hesitating as I silently questioned, "What I am supposed to do here again?" Instead of being seen as a seasoned executive with a lot to offer, I played right into the stereotype by not being fast enough with the technology. Not being well enough prepared. I was "dinosaur-ish."

ADAPTATION IS THE KEY TO INFLUENCE

The lesson here is you can't just approach everyone in the same way. The more you look at the style and the particular pressures on a person, the more you can adjust your delivery accordingly.

Remember, this is not a suggestion that you act in a disingenuous manner. This is a recommendation that you stop and ask yourself, "Am I approaching this properly? Before I go charging in there with my idea/my request, how can I pitch it in a way most likely to get a positive response?"

In Chapter Three, we talked about stepping back and checking your work. Same idea, but in this case, it's about checking your *approach*.

We all have different personality characteristics and preferences. When you drill down and understand yours, you can turn that knowledge into a benefit. Capitalize on what works well, and learn to compensate where there is an impediment. Approach your work relationships with open eyes, and observe the styles of people you're working with. Is your style a natural fit with theirs? Or do you need to adapt in order for your relationships to function more smoothly?

The world has been adapting since the beginning of time. It works.

TEAM UP WITH YOUR COWORKERS

Don't overlook an opportunity to enlist the talents of others to help you overcome obstacles. For example, if you're nervous about addressing a group of higher-ups at work, ask a coworker to assist you. Perhaps they could present with you. For many people who struggle with speaking in front of a crowd, something as simple as a question from a "friendly face" in the audience can go a long way toward calming their nerves, even if the entire meeting is virtual.

Knowing your strengths, weaknesses, preferences, and tolerances—and being aware of those of the people around you—enables you to leverage those complementary assets for joint success.

Having a willing coworker who'll assist you as needed can get you through some very difficult situations, well beyond a simple presentation. I was once part of a department that needed to get the entire company on board with using our services. The company also had a complex hierarchy in which a person's job title didn't always reflect their level of influence. Our whole team was new, with a lot of territory to cover in a short time.

The most social, people-oriented guy on our team became our ambassador. He became our "advance man." Part of his role was to walk the hallways, meet people, and introduce himself and our team. He would hand out his business card and explain what we did. He got to know who was who, asked a few questions, and paved the way for bigger meetings and more engagement.

Business books talk about the value of getting support from the people at the top of an organization when you want to make change. But if you engage the lower- to mid-levels of a company as well, you get the momentum and power needed to effect major change quickly. While I was meeting with senior executives, this advance man put a friendly face on our department and our services and got much deeper into the organization, helping people understand who we were and what we were trying to accomplish.

In every company, there are a handful of people who make things happen—and the CEO isn't necessarily one of them. The challenge is identifying who they are. This process helped us do that.

KEY POINTS

- Your professional toolkit should include some knowledge of work styles and corporate culture.

- One way to increase your effectiveness is to understand your own preferences when it comes to the way you work and adjust the actions you would naturally take to get the job done.

- Everyone around you has a preferred style. In order to get your message across, you may need to adjust your natural actions to fit the styles of the people you work with.

QUESTIONS FOR THE READER

1. What are your preferences? What work style are you drawn to naturally?

2. Pick someone in the organization with whom you need to interact. Observe their style. Do they approach work the same way you do? How is their style similar to yours, and how is it different?

3. What can you do differently at work that might make your ideas better received by management, coworkers, or people who work for you?

CHAPTER FIVE

LET'S MAKE A DEAL

A negotiation is a discussion between people trying to reach an agreement. It's the art of getting someone to agree to what you want—the process of persuading someone to support your ideas.

Throughout my career in procurement and supply chain, I negotiated a lot of deals. Anyone doing my job would have to be a decent negotiator. But that's not necessarily the kind of negotiating I'm talking about here. Most people will never have to create a business contract. But every day, at work and at home, every one of us winds up trying to come to an agreement with someone else in some way. Whether you are an eighteen-year-old looking for a curfew extension or a forty-eight-year-old looking for a raise, you can benefit from being a better negotiator.

It might not be in your job description, but at work, you are constantly negotiating. When you take a new position, you want your employer to agree to what you want: starting salary, vacation time, and maybe your benefits. Later on, you deal with bosses and colleagues, maybe even clients or vendors. You negotiate the date that a work assignment will be completed; you may negotiate with your manager to get some resources to help you; you try to sell your ideas to decision makers. Negotiating moves your ideas forward and gets you what you want, so the more negotiating tools you have, the more effective you will be.

When there's a lot of churn, the ability to negotiate is an important skill to acquire. Many times, successfully influencing someone was directly tied to my success or failure at work. But even more important, I often had to convince people to give me a job, promote me, or choose me for a project I wanted to be on. The person who said "you get what you negotiate" was right.

Effecting change involves negotiating. According to professional mediator Tammy Lenski, the reality is that "at work, pretty much every conversation is a negotiation."[2]

2   Kim Lankford, "Negotiation Tips from a Professional Mediator," *Monster*, accessed May 22, 2017, https://www.monster.com/career-advice/article/negotiation-tips-from-a-mediator.

She's right. A basic understanding of the elements of negotiation will help you in your day-to-day conversations with your employer, your customers, and your internal customers, because it's all about getting people to agree to what you want.

There are dozens of courses, podcasts, books, and webinars that teach the basics of negotiation, so it's silly for me to try to do that here. Instead, this chapter provides some highlights and a few helpful stories from the frontlines. It focuses on the nuances—some things to try that have come into my toolkit after years of being in the trenches. These are techniques I picked up by working with talented negotiators.

Because we're all in different situations, not all the examples in this chapter will directly apply to you. But keep an open mind, because you'll find that there are nuggets of wisdom in all of them and sooner or later most of them will be of use.

REMEMBER CHAPTER FOUR: IT'S NOT ABOUT YOU; IT'S ABOUT THEM

Winston Churchill once said, "When you're twenty, you care what everything thinks, when you're 40 you stop caring what everyone thinks, when you're 60 you realize no one was ever thinking about you in the first place..."

Getting what you want requires you to put yourself in the shoes of the other person—thinking about their receptivity and their reactions. That's what Chapter Four was all about.

Building on that thought, any negotiator will tell you that you will be more successful in a situation if you can match styles with the people you're dealing with.[3] It's a key to getting things done. Negotiating depends on your communication skills, and even a small change, such as altering the cadence of your voice to match that of the person to whom you're speaking, can make a difference in how your message is received. You can establish trust more quickly if you put that person at ease by letting them know, in subtle ways, that the two of you have similarities and share common ground. If they speak quickly, pick up your pace. If they are measured and deliberate, slow down. Reduce the points of difference between your styles.

Matching postures or physical movements can be helpful, too. Observe how the people around you stand, move, and gesture; then, make sure your physical motion complements theirs. You're not mimicking someone with bad intent; you're adjusting your style to make them feel at ease, to make them more receptive to your message. The key is to mirror the other person just enough to make them

---

3   David J. Lieberman, *Never Be Lied to Again: How to Get the Truth in 5 Minutes or Less in Any Conversation or Situation* (New York: St. Martin's Griffin, 1999).

comfortable. Don't gesticulate wildly with someone who keeps themselves very still, and don't be stiff or "wooden" with someone with a bigger body style. Level the playing field in terms of communication, and you're likely to be perceived more openly and get more accomplished.

Remember my coffee with the COO described in the last chapter? He was visibly uncomfortable until I scaled down my naturally enthusiastic demeanor. We were only having a friendly networking meeting; think of how unsuccessful I would have been without adapting to his style if I were actually trying to get him to agree to something.

TACKLE THE HARD STUFF

Proudly, I presented the outline of a contract to my boss for his review. This was my very first time doing a deal on my own, without his watchful eye. He read it, made a few notes, and handed it back.

"You forgot the most important part," he said. "This agreement lays out all the things our company and the supplier plan to do. But what if something goes wrong? What if a new management team comes in with a new strategy? What if one of us runs into financial difficulties and can't proceed? What if the market changes? You forgot one of the most important things—to negotiate the hard stuff."

He added that the best time to work out a plan to handle future problems is at the beginning, when you're still friends—not at the end, when you're mad at each other. He advised to always negotiate the hard stuff first.

That's the part we tend to skip over, right? We have great intentions when we agree to buy or sell something, but we get embarrassed to talk about what happens if things don't go as we planned. And we often feel funny about money, not always asking for the fine details that can make a difference in how much things cost or what kind of service is available.

A friend of mine runs a successful law firm in Brooklyn. At one point, he was frustrated because, while he was attracting many clients, he subsequently had a hard time making them pay the invoices he sent once the work was done. He asked for my advice.

"Well," I said, "when we take our dog to the vet, the vet first offers a few options for treatment, and each option has a different cost. She structures it so that we discuss the different options and make a choice before treatment. That way, there are no surprises when the bill comes, because we've all agreed on what we're going to pay. Why don't you have that conversation with your clients up front? Be clear about what the services are and what they cost, and make sure you both agree before you take them on as a client." He implemented my suggestion and was thrilled with the results. Every time I see him, he tells me what a difference that advice made to his business.

Another friend, Tandra, does a lot of negotiating. She makes detailed lists of what could go wrong in the course of a deal. She also schedules point-by-point conversations with the other side that meticulously cover potential problems and solutions. She leaves no stone unturned in her preparation. I watched a situation in which she negotiated a big, global deal for many months, which involved doing separate agreements one country at a time—literally working her way around the globe, learning the nuances of contracts in each country. Suddenly, a new executive team announced a different direction. She had to undo everything, which normally would have cost the company a lot of money and a lot of litigation. But her thoughtful conversations about what could go wrong at every step created a map that laid a path for her to follow when she had to undo the agreement, country by country.

A final example of negotiating the hard stuff first happens when you're in the job market. You're excited to be getting hired at a great new job, and your future employer is happy because they've filled an opening. All is well. *This* is the time to negotiate the items you're afraid to talk about. If the company has a severance policy, you can get it embedded into your offer letter—or ask for something a little better—just in case there's some churn up ahead. Maybe you are leaving a job with four weeks of vacation, and the policy at the new company is to start at two. Or you'd like to adjust your hours to help with the daycare pickup. Negotiate it. Said more simply, just ask for it. Then, make sure you get it in writing. Do it up front, when you are both happy with each other, when you're both still "friends."

BE NICE

While you're experimenting with your business style, don't lose sight of who you are as a person.

Some people are mean. I had a boss who was one of the old-fashioned, corporate vice presidents who made people quake in fear. Twice, he was actually fired and still showed up to work the following week, and no one had the nerve to tell him to leave. It worked for him because he had the presence, confidence, and arrogance to pull it off.

Don't try this, though. The world is a different place now, and if he were still working, he'd never have made it past his first 360-degree feedback session.

A business partner frequently spoke about an executive in a big financial services firm. She favored long meetings with coworkers and partners that dragged on and on.

Whenever she was the most senior person in the room, she'd order a pitcher of cold water and a single glass, sipping from it as the meeting went on and never offering the water to anyone else. Why—to make herself look more important? What did she think she would gain by making everyone else uncomfortable? Did that help her secure allies or build anyone's trust? She wasn't eliminating distractions—she was creating one.

I spent years trying to get my kids and their friends to be afraid of me. No luck. Mean doesn't work for me—everyone just chuckles. I mentioned this to a mentor who gave me some advice that is still relevant today. He said, "I get great results. Everyone thinks I'm a tiger who rips people to shreds. But why do that? You may be fighting hard for an idea or something you want, but once you've won the debate, you still need to have an ongoing relationship with the other person. I couldn't be nicer. Not a pushover, just a nice guy. Why not?"

J. Paul Getty was the founder of Getty Oil, and in the 1960s, he was the world's wealthiest private citizen. Getty was a well-known miser with a string of relationship failures, but his business strategy was similar to that of my mentor. He said, "You must never try to make all the money that's in a deal. Let the other fellow make some money too, because if you have a reputation for always making all the money, you won't have many deals."

Whether you are buying a car in your personal life or leading a team in your professional life, you'll be a whole lot
happier if you resolve to treat people decently.

ESTABLISH CREDIBILITY WITH ENVIRONMENTAL LANGUAGE

How do you establish credibility when you don't fit the
norm, when you're not what people expect?

For example, I entered college as one of five women in
an entry class of over 400 people. Many assumed we
were merely shopping for husbands—and told us so. Also,
I'm a little shy, never the most outgoing person in the
room. And as the years went by, I became one of the older
employees in the companies I worked in. Always someone who didn't fit the mold. How to get people to take
me seriously? Surprisingly, the answer came via a huge
laminate of my professional engineering license, given
to me as a present. The giver, a former business associate,
never dreamed he was providing me with a powerful tool
to assist my future success—and I didn't realize it, either,
at first. It hung prominently in my office, right near the
table where everyone sat for meetings. The license was
eventually joined by a certificate for post-graduate work
that I did at a respected university. Newcomers—mostly
men—never failed to notice and comment. You might
call this tactic "environmental language"—much like

body language, it gets the point across without saying anything. Those framed documents showed that I was accomplished in my field, despite what other people's preconceived notions might be.

Putting your credentials on display is harder to do in an open-workspace environment, and it may not translate well within the culture of some companies. You may not even have a formal corporate workspace; you may be home-based. That's OK. You can compensate by making sure that your online presence is complete and that someone doing a search on you is going to find your education, accomplishments, thought leadership, etc., if they look for it. Don't be reticent—in the absence of physical space, virtual space is all you have to get your message across, so you really need to use it. Your reputation as an accomplished individual can carry a lot of weight in getting people to listen to you.

One year, my brother-in-law gave me a fuzzy, leopard clipboard for Christmas. I stopped carrying a black notebook to meetings and started clipping sheets of paper to this crazy thing. Why? It sent a subtle message that I wasn't afraid to think unconventionally.

What can you do to subtly convey your competence?

THINK BEFORE YOU LEAP INTO THAT VIDEOCONFERENCE

Face-to-face communication is ideal for establishing relationships, but as technology has evolved, more conferences, meetings, and negotiations take place via Skype or similar tools. Learn how to use them properly. There are plenty of YouTube videos out there that will teach you how to improve your Skype experience, from the right lighting to controlling background noise.

At the very least, set up your own station, monitor, and surrounding environment so you can stay "in the moment" and are not distracted. Removing distractions from the person on the opposite end is more difficult, but it's important to do that as well. We never know what's competing for the other person's attention that we can't see. They may have their phone in front of them but hidden from view. They could be reading email on a split screen while we're making a key point.

I learned this lesson the hard way, during a pitch I was making to a group of executives who were deciding whether to hire me. There were technical problems on their end. They could see me, but I couldn't see them. (Maybe that was on purpose?) So I was on camera, trying to look energetic and engaged as I stared at a blank screen. The video flickered back on unexpectedly for a moment, and I realized that everyone on the other end was doing something else, and they were barely paying attention to my pitch at all.

How often does that happen when you're on the phone? You're talking, and you can hear the click, click, click of people tapping on their keyboards.

The fact is that people aren't good listeners; there are way too many distractions competing for their attention. What do you do? Develop a "remote" strategy. If you have an important point to make, plan ahead and think about ways to get the kind of engagement from a person that you would if you were sitting in the same room. Give them something worth listening to. Ask more questions. Not just yes and no or multiple-choice questions, but open-ended questions that require them to think and provide detailed answers. Engage them in conversation. Consider two or three brief calls rather than a long call where your counterparts are more likely to multitask or become distracted. And whenever possible, be there in person. Energy is difficult to convey when technology is the third "person" at the table.

LOCATION, LOCATION, LOCATION

We've covered how you can use your personal space to build your credibility, and how videoconferencing can have pitfalls. There's another option, which is meeting face-to-face. Although declining in frequency, there is great value in actually being in the same room. Much easier to establish rapport. Less chance of distraction. Better opportunity to get your point across. There is no substitute for actually being there.

This requires some strategizing as well. If you're complaining about costs, bringing someone you're negotiating with to a lavish headquarters building is a bad idea. On the other hand, if you're trying to do a business deal with someone who is new and might not be well acquainted with your company, bringing them to your site might help them get energized about supporting your business—particularly if they are able to meet an executive or two.

Going to the site of the third party you are speaking with is often a good idea if you are trying to get more information about the company, culture, hierarchy, etc. By keeping your eyes open—and maybe meeting a few people yourself—you can increase what you know about your partner. There's no single right answer, but it's an opportunity that gets easily forgotten in this world of working remotely.

The same applies if you are asking for something within your company. Don't hide behind emails that may get overlooked or quickly scanned or misinterpreted. There's a lot to be said for eye contact, most importantly that you have the other person's attention. However brief your interaction might be, at least you know they are listening to you.

The person you want to meet with is busy? Don't try to set up an hour-long meeting—distill what you want to fifteen minutes. That's a lot easier to get. And if your message intrigues them, they'll extend the meeting.

THE PEOPLE YOU'RE DEALING WITH: WHAT'S IN IT FOR THEM?

A group of us were preparing to negotiate a tough deal. Because of manufacturing constraints, we had no choice but to work with a supplier with whom there was a bad history and, as a result, a very contentious relationship.

The team prepared for our meetings in all the usual ways. Our objectives were clear, industry trends were analyzed, and financial elements were understood.

The revelation came when the *personal* aspects were considered. Someone created an organizational chart of the company with which we would be dealing, and we all shared information about what we knew about the individuals on the other side. As a clear picture emerged, we came to the conclusion that one of the key people was under significant pressure to get this deal done. He had previous issues with subpar performance. We researched his challenges and his failures, and we concluded that he needed a success. His job probably depended on it. Once we identified him as the weak link in the chain, we targeted him and worked hard to give him a way to make a deal with us. We brought ideas to him that he could then forward within his company, thereby effectively making him our advocate. In effect, we also helped him become the hero of the deal and helped his reputation with his own company.

This was a new way of getting prepared, but now, I do it all the time. *Who are the key players? What can we learn about them? Why would this person want to make a deal with us? What's in it for them? What can we do to change their minds?* Answer these questions, and then figure out how to capitalize on what you discover. Everyone can win.

Identifying personal situations works with whatever idea you're trying to sell. Don't go to your boss for a raise when he's under pressure to reduce costs. If you have an idea to improve efficiency, pitch it to the person feeling squeezed from the bad process in place.

Chapter Four got us thinking about individuals and their styles. A few pages ago, we reflected on how it could help us negotiate. This rounds out the picture by looking at the personal circumstances those people are in. The two elements together give you what you need to know to get listened to.

UNDERSTAND THE GOAL

We've also talked about relentless preparation. Here's a related example, where focusing on a clear, simple goal (obtained by doing the right preparation) saved a potentially disastrous meeting.

The senior vice president of operations was a nice guy who was well known and revered in the industry. He was approached by a former colleague about a joint venture, and on the basis of past partnerships, he was predisposed to do the deal. His team didn't think he had done his homework, and we were afraid that he was making the decision based on emotion, not information. As good as he was, he relied heavily on relationships, sometimes with the assumption that the details would just work themselves out.

So we asked the chief accountant to give us the current manufacturing cost. *One number*—this is what it costs us to make this today. If the other guy quotes a lower number, it's a good deal. If he quotes a higher number, it's not a good deal—at least not until we negotiate it down. We wrote it down on a piece of paper. One number. The difference between a good deal and a bad deal.

We gave our boss the paper.

When we met the people from the other company for dinner, we saw the SVP place the paper on his lap and discretely cover it with his dinner napkin. As expected, the conversation eventually got to price. When the other party mentioned the price they would charge, our boss picked up the napkin, glanced at the number, and replaced the napkin. We could see him flinch just the tiniest bit, and we could imagine his mind turning over, as if to say, *Oh no, I must have misunderstood. That can't possibly be the right number because it's so much lower than what the other guy just quoted.* He seemed to be absorbing the shocking information as he lifted and replaced the napkin to see the number on that paper three or four times.

It's a comical image in retrospect, but the moment was tense. Would we have gone all the way and done a bad deal if we didn't have that information at that very moment? No, certainly that information would have come out at some point. But did we save ourselves a lot of unnecessary work and save him some embarrassment by getting the facts straight first and distilling the decision to a single number? Yes, we did.

DON'T ASK SOMEONE TO CHANGE THEIR MIND

Have you ever been in a situation where someone says

"no" to you—over and over again? We spend a lot of time trying to get people to change their minds, yet research shows that people rarely do so. Once they've taken a position—especially if they've taken it publicly—people get attached to that decision. Without even realizing it, they "stand behind" their response and are unlikely to change. Why should they?

In situations like this, your job is to find new facts that lead to a different conclusion, so they can effectively answer a different question. You have to provide them with information they didn't know previously. This way, you're putting some power back into their hands, instead of making them feel as if they're being asked to capitulate. Offer them new numbers, new facts, new observations, and new evidence to support your position.

The "Captain Cook Method" below describes one way this can work.

THE CAPTAIN COOK METHOD

This method was created after a vacation in Polynesia, where an anthropologist lectured about the region and its history. She told my group that when James Cook was searching for Easter Island, he sailed to the spot indicated by the rather imprecise navigational tools of the time. And all he saw was water.

According to the story, Cook sailed his ship in ever-widening circles until he saw land. I can't verify the story's historical accuracy, but it made an impact on me in terms of the corporate environment. Cook tackled the problem by circling and circling it until it was solved.

Fast-forward a few months. I was in a new office and a new job with lots of ideas on ways I could create some Positive Disruption at my new employer. But I had to get buy-in from the business leaders, which was not going to be an easy thing. It was a successful company. No particular burning platform. Then I remembered the Captain Cook story.

First, I sat with a few trusted teammates, and we drew a circle. Then, we wrote the names of each department and department head on our list around the circle. There was a name at twelve o'clock, another name at one o'clock, and so on. Starting at twelve o'clock, my team and I worked clockwise, meeting various leaders, making our pitch on how we could improve things, and asking for their approval to proceed. If someone pushed back, we just thanked them and moved on. We didn't worry, and just kept plugging away until someone said, "OK." After going around the circle once, we had met all the business heads and had approvals to proceed with a handful of projects. So we worked hard on delivering great results.

Then, once we had some successes under our belts, we

started back around the circle to the people who had pushed back in the past. This time, it was a different kind of conversation. This time, we had some successes to talk about and better ideas on what we could do for their unit. The conversations changed the second time around, and so did the responses. We had a better "product" to sell because we had more concrete examples, and we received more positive responses because our clients had new information.

There were still a few holdouts, and eventually there was a third round. This time, the conversation was different yet again. It was more along the lines of, "We've just completed x, y, and z. Now it's time to work with your group."

We stopped asking permission, because we didn't have to anymore. We had a track record; we had credibility. The other party had new facts, new information. It was a different conversation.

ONE RIOT, ONE RANGER

Have you ever noticed how people travel in packs to meetings? How often multiple people from the same department spend most of their workdays together—so much so that it's not always clear where one person's responsibilities end and another's start?

There's a comfort level in having a buddy with you, in having someone with whom you can relax, with whom you can toss around ideas when the meeting is done. But staffs are smaller than they used to be, workloads heavier. The days of big travel budgets are gone, and on the rare occasion when people actually meet face-to-face, there may be a single representative where there used to be a team. This new development comes with drawbacks, but you can make it work to your advantage.

I was once sent abroad to participate in important meetings regarding a merger with a rival. Walking into the conference room, I was the only person representing the American team for our company, while our rivals had a large group glaring at me. Calling my boss in a panic, I asked him, "What am I going to do? I'm so outnumbered!" His response? "You're going to remember the motto of the Texas Rangers," he said. "*One riot, one ranger*. Get back in there!"

Being alone worked. When there was pressure to make a commitment I didn't feel good about, the response could be, "Well, you know, I really need to check with my leadership. This is a decision that affects too many other people." When it came to something I was comfortable with, I could go ahead and agree to it. It enhanced my role within the dealmaking because I was perceived as someone who needed to be taken seriously—after all, they sent me by myself! No one else needed to know that it was an accident.

We all have our work "posse"—our team of peers with whom we spend our days and are very comfortable. We like to work together and naturally form teams when a big task has to get done. Heck, I worked with one company where you could fill a stadium with all the people who were there for "input."

But my suggestion here is that you think about it. As we said in the prior chapter, do what is necessary not what comes naturally. Scary as it is, having a single "face" may often be a good tactic. And if nothing else, it's an efficient one.

LEARN LESSONS FROM YOUR MISTAKES

Things can fall apart for the strangest reasons. No matter how well you prepare, something you didn't consider can throw a wrench in your work. Failure can be a great teacher, though, so learn from your failures and try not to repeat them.

A memorable failed negotiation happened when our company was in the middle of purchasing a significant piece of technology. The cost was outrageous, and we were trying to find ways to bring it down. My team had been involved in the negotiations for a while and done all our homework—or so we thought. At a big meeting between the decision makers, our brand-new CEO and the other company's CEO shook hands warmly. They hugged because they knew each other well. And we had no idea they were practically neighbors. Face-to-face in that room, we couldn't come to an agreement because our CEO wasn't going to push, and neither man was going to concede anything to the other.

How did we miss that? Epic fail, in front of the CEO. Ouch. Didn't let that happen again.

KEEP PERSPECTIVE

At work, people are under a lot of stress, and it's not uncommon for emotions to run high. Don't let the pressure get the best of you. If you plan ahead, you might come up with a solution for relieving tension so that the problem of the moment can be resolved.

An early mentor had a brilliant technique for "humanizing" tense conversations. He worked in a ground-floor, corner office with big windows overlooking a beautiful lake. The company used a border collie named Duncan to help control bothersome migrating Canada geese that sometimes chased employees who walked too close by. My boss kept a plastic dog bone in his desk that, when pressed, emitted a dog's bark. Whenever negotiations became particularly heated, he secretly pressed the button. The tension would immediately dissipate as everyone looked around for the source. He would tell them about the geese and the company's collie, everyone would go to the window to look for Duncan, and the whole atmosphere would shift, offering everyone a breather. A little sneaky, perhaps, but that momentary diversion allowed everyone to take a deep breath and press the restart button—whether they realized it or not.

That same person taught me that when you're pushing hard, make sure what you're fighting for is worth fighting for. If you're digging in your heels, consider the larger picture of what's at stake and decide whether you should dig in or reconsider your position. Make sure you haven't gotten so caught up in the desire to win that you are pushing for something you don't really need.

On another occasion, four of us were on the way to a big presentation, in front of an audience partially composed of people who didn't agree with our program or our perspectives. We donned sunglasses, took our briefcases, and walked to the meeting in midtown Manhattan looking like characters from *Men in Black*. It was a great way to work off the tension and make us feel confident.

Maybe you've read about the TED talk given by Amy

Cuddy about the Power Pose, and you stand with your hands on your hips to gain confidence before an important meeting. Or you meditate. Whatever works for you to dissipate negative thoughts and focus forward.

I'M NOT A NEGOTIATOR—WHY DO I NEED TO KNOW ANY OF THIS?

Ah, but you are. Remember the quote at the start of this chapter, that every conversation is a negotiation. Think about the number of times you ask for something, the number of times you try to get your idea listened to. Maybe the Captain Cook Method will come in handy the next time you have to set priorities; instead of tackling the biggest project first, perhaps you tackle the easiest so that you can show some quick results. Maybe you use humor to diffuse a tense situation or understand the personal pressures your coworkers are under and how they might be influencing their reactions and judgements. Or you update your social media profile to make sure it conveys you as the professional you want the world to see.

This chapter and the few before were about scoping out the terrain, thinking about how to approach people with ideas. The next one, Chapter Six, is about taking all of these tools, finding ideas, and using them to create Positive Disruptions in your workplace.

KEY POINTS

- Every conversation is a negotiation.

- Instead of asking someone to change their mind, give them new information that reframes what you're asking them to do.

- Put the other person at ease. Be alert for cues as to what makes them uncomfortable.

- Negotiate the hard stuff first. Think about the hard stuff, the sticky points that you may feel shy or awkward bringing up to someone. Push yourself to ask the question and get it resolved early in the relationship, when everyone is on their best behavior.

QUESTIONS FOR THE READER

1. Which of these new ideas and approaches for negotiating make sense in your situation?

2. How can you use "environmental language" to get the message across that you are competent and capable?

3. Think of a situation when you proposed a change at work and the company did not agree to implement it. What would you do differently if you had another chance?

CHAPTER SIX

READY, SET, GO (BETTER TO BE A DISRUPTOR THAN A DISRUPTEE)

Some of us are paid to go to work every day and do the same repetitive tasks, day in and day out. Tough. Boring. And soon to be replaced by robots.

But all of us can use our brainpower and ideas to make improvements. They don't have to be billion-dollar ideas. They can be little changes that don't take any monetary investment at all. Positive changes—Positive Disruptions.

WHAT EXACTLY IS DISRUPTION, AGAIN?

According to Harvard professor Clayton Christensen, along with two other authors, "'Disruption' describes a process whereby a smaller company with fewer resources is able to successfully challenge established incumbent businesses."[4] Companies, as they grow, focus on what's profitable and on their largest customers, figuring out ways to make tweaks to their products—whether the customers want them or not. Then, along comes a disruptor. For example, while many hotel chains courted the business customer and high-end vacation traveler, Airbnb came along to serve an ignored segment of the market, the budget traveler. The more people use Airbnb, the bigger a disruptor it becomes.

This is analogous to the situation *within* a company. How many times have you heard someone say, "That's the way we do things here"? Companies invest in technologies and consultants that create ways of doing things, and employees repeat them day in and day out. They are taught a certain way and don't stop to question or consider positive changes as time goes by.

Disruption is change. It shakes things up. It creates new processes. Maybe a site closes and jobs are eliminated.

---

4   Clayton M. Christensen, Michael E. Raynor, and Rory McDonald, "What Is Disruptive Innovation?" *Harvard Business Review*, Dec. 2015, accessed Aug. 14, 2017, https://hbr.org/2015/12/what-is-disruptive-innovation.

Maybe you start doing something differently than you had in the past—or stop doing a task altogether because it is no longer necessary. One thing is for sure: contemporary corporate life doesn't reward people who keep their heads down. Companies need employees who understand Positive Disruption—why it's necessary, how to adapt to it, and even how to create it.

Positive Disruption is positive change that you can see and feel. It is change that results in a good benefit for your company. It means doing things differently for an ultimate result that you're proud of. A software modification that makes your company's servers run more efficiently is not a disruption, because it happens behind the scenes and you don't see or feel it. But if you live near a toll road, you may have seen the toll collectors disappear, replaced by electronic tolling methods. That's a Positive Disruption for the motorist. Although you have the momentary pain of acquiring an E-ZPass account, in the end, there is a transformation to a smoother, faster journey.

In previous chapters, you learned how to create a backup plan so that you can weather the churn that comes when your work life is disrupted by events outside your control. We talked about how to identify the culture and characters in your workplace. You also learned a few solid negotiating techniques, so you've got some skills and have figured out who's who and how to approach them to sell your ideas.

You've embraced the churn. Now, maybe it's time to create some Positive Disruption of your own.

You can be at the forefront of positive change. You are always, *always* in a better position as a disrupter than you are as a "disruptee." The art of Positive Disruption is a prized skill, so mastering it will make you a valued employee at the right company.

PAST SUCCESSES CAN BE AN OBSTACLE TO FUTURE DISRUPTION

Ironically, many companies that were first to invest in technology are now saddled with out-of-date systems that no longer align with current processes in the rest of the world. Technologies that were cutting-edge fifteen years ago are now ancient. They might require teams of people and lots of investment to be adjusted or be so complicated that an infrequent user needs a refresher course every time they log on. Today, being an early adopter is only good until the next big innovation comes long. Then, you're prehistoric.

Processes are implemented because they serve a purpose at the time they are put in place. They may have outlived their usefulness, but no one notices because they become part of the day-to-day fabric of how things get done. So people keep following them. How many reports are created at your company that no one looks at? Question them. Is the information available in another format somewhere, and is it even necessary to track it? The number and size of the tools required for smooth operations are shrinking, but sometimes, companies hold on to old systems and processes because no one really owns them—so no one takes responsibility for getting rid of them. As a new employee in one company, every person I met with—as they explained how things worked in this firm—said, "I have no idea how things happen in other places, but this is our way." They just kept doing the same thing every day, until the time came that the company was in peril because it had been years since anyone had made a real improvement.

Sometimes, the solution is a big one—an expensive overhaul or business transformation. But small changes count as well. They help establish a mindset, an environment of embracing disruption.

Ask yourself, "How long does it take to process an order, get a sale, or deliver a product? How could my own job be more effective or efficient?" Often, you'll find that it's been a long time since someone has looked at the way things get done, and they have no idea how much employee time and company resources are consumed.

Early in my career, I was given the task of calculating how long it took to make a particular type of wound-care product. The primary machines ran 700 units a minute, but it took nearly ninety days from the time the materials arrived at the dock door to the time the completed packages were on their way to the customer because of wasted steps and inventory as well as other inefficiencies. That little measurement set off a whirlwind of disruption at my employer. Having the facts at hand helped our leadership get the investment to rework the process.

In their book, *Finance Unleashed*, Magnus Lind and Kelly Barner point out that value can be extracted from support activities as well.[5] They cite that Toyota reports taking just eighteen hours to make a customized car, and they note that it can take up to forty-eight hours to send the cross-border payment for the car. Think of all the steps that the payment process involves, and all the opportunity to make positive changes.

On a smaller scale, do you produce any reports that no one ever asks a question about? Keep your eyes open and see what time, cost, and operational streamlining you can bring to something in your work or your company. Be the problem solver who brings Positive Disruption to the job, and your work will be valued.

---

5   Magnus Lind and Kelly Barner, *Finance Unleashed: Leveraging the CFO for Innovation* (New York: Palgrave Macmillan, 2017).

DISRUPT FOR "EASY"

Look around your company. The very people struggling to buy a headset or input travel expenses for approval are buying shoes on Zappos and diapers online at lunchtime. They book Airbnbs in Iceland and wire money to their kids at college with a few clicks of their mouse. They know how easy booking business travel and logging expenses *should* be. That's because, in their personal lives, they are able to use whatever technology they can afford and whatever apps they can download that make life easier.

Lunch is over, and people start yelling because they're going to waste half a day trying to approve a purchase, or complete an employee evaluation, or get reimbursed for their business travel. In their business lives, they're constrained to using whatever system exists internally—whatever system was invested in a dozen years ago. A few years ago, Christian Lanng, the CEO and cofounder of Tradeshift, tweeted about one of the big players in supply chain software, observing "They don't have customers, they have prisoners." That describes many situations. The big investment is made, and you're stuck with it until a disruptor comes along and figures a way out. Maybe that disruptor is you.

Challenging the status quo and causing Positive Disruption mean dealing with this kind of problem. It's about looking at the tasks that take people away from doing what they were hired to do or that slow people down—creatively looking for ways to automate or eliminate things that don't add value.

THE BIG IDEAS

There are lots of big ideas out there. Artificial intelligence. Blockchain technology. Big Data. Robotics. The internet of things. New concepts, all of which are in their infancy.

Some companies have the size and breadth to partner with the creators of these big ideas. Walmart can partner with its food suppliers and with IBM to use blockchain technology to track the movement of food around the globe, making it easier and faster to identify the source if a problem is found. The Department of Defense uses artificial intelligence to assist its procurement process; its 1,087-page manual is a challenge for humans to effectively manage without help.

The journey to big invention can be a long one. Sizeable investments need to be made, and sizeable benefit needs to occur to justify the expense. The benefit may come many years out. It's important work, but a small or mid-size firm often doesn't have the mass or the capital to invest.

That's OK. If you create a culture of Positive Disruption, a culture in which change is embraced, you can still see benefits and still see positive change, one step at a time. The more changes you make, the more it becomes accepted. And a path lined with small changes can create a mindset that leads to a big idea.

HOW DOES THIS WORK FOR A SMALLER BUSINESS LIKE THE ONE I'M IN?

Remember from the beginning of this chapter that disruptors in the classic definition look for markets that aren't being serviced. Within a business, disruptors question the status quo and find new, better ways to do things—or maybe not do them at all.

Amazon started by selling books online, commencing a disruption that began with brick-and-mortar bookstores and transformed retailing across the world. The company filled a void that people arguably didn't realize existed. Today, its market cap approaches $1 trillion.

On the other side of the US, Christian Iannucci works on a different scale but is a disruptor nonetheless. Inspired by Amazon and by companies like Uber, TaskRabbit, and Shyp that were leading the trend in on-demand services, he founded Doorbell Barbers. He saw the opportunity for on-call barber or salon services outside of the traditional brick-and-mortar model, especially with an increasing population of seniors and home-bound individuals. His company relies on independent contractors, third-party SaaS (software as a service), and low-cost, online, targeted advertising to attract customers. As a result, he can get professionals to work where his clients are, instead of the other way around, and is able to put a higher percentage of fees in the pockets of the service providers who work with his company.

A regular person can contribute lots of positive ideas to their company. You don't need special training. What you do need to do is look around you, learn how others have dealt with challenges, and bring the ideas to your company. You don't have to be an inventor—you can be an adaptor. Here are a few more examples of Positive Disruption. Maybe one of them will spur an idea for you.

STOP DOING WHAT NO LONGER WORKS

Say you're going on an international trip for work and need an adaptor, or your wireless mouse stops working and needs to be replaced. What do you do? You probably have to go through a process to decide exactly what you want, put a requisition into some kind of system, get it approved, and wait for it to arrive.

One mega-technology company solved this by creating the *Tech Stop*, which is a storage area containing commonly requested technology items. Employees who need a piece of equipment simply visit their Tech Stop and pick it up without any bureaucracy attached—no requisitions, approvals, or waiting. The company recognized that outdated processes burden the entire system, not to mention the lost productivity and hit to employee morale caused by forcing people to wait to get the tools they need to do their jobs. They measure activity and make adjustments as needed, changing the rules, for example, when headsets were moving out faster than expected.

Other companies have tried using storage units that work like vending machines for employees when they need to replenish small, frequently used items.

One of the first examples in this book was championed by a travel manager who realized that documents were being express-mailed daily between sites that were less than a mile apart. A dozen years after that took place, I attended a dynamic presentation by an executive at a biopharma company, someone known in his profession as a champion disruptor. When asked to give examples of his successes, the first one that he touted was a similar situation, when his company stopped sending physical documents to physicians and hospitals around the world and automated the process instead. Not only did they save money on express mail, it turned out that even the remote sites were also more automated than they had perceived, and it was a huge timesaver for the receivers, who had been laboriously keying the files into their own systems, page by page. The first of these examples took no monetary investment at all; in the second, it was minor. Both were Positive Disruptions in which the companies stopped doing something.

ADAPT SOMETHING FROM ONE USE TO ANOTHER

Look around at the little pieces of technology that make your life easier at home—can they help you at work? How can you take the concept and apply it differently?

There are five buttons on the cabinet door in my laundry room—five Amazon Dash Buttons. The Amazon Dash Button is another disruptive bit of technology that allows customers to connect a small "button" through Wi-Fi to Amazon Prime and make automatic purchases of household or office items they buy regularly by simply pushing a button. Push the button, and the item you want arrives two days later. Although I use it for Ziploc baggies and laundry detergent, think of the uses in a small office for items like cleaning supplies, pantry items, even copier paper. What if you identified small, frequent transactions and searched for solutions like this?

FOCUS ON THE DESIRED END RESULT

There's a book on leaders called *First, Break all the Rules*.[6] That title speaks volumes to me. Sometimes, we forget which regulations must be followed because of the legal or moral implications of not doing so, and which corporate rules are there because that's the way it is.

A former classmate has been granted sixty patents in the field of supercomputers. He and his team create some disruption of their own on the path to innovation. He explained, "I'd like to tell you about our creative process. Basically, we would come up with our idea and work on it awhile. When we had a good sense of what we wanted to test next, we'd make up a list of equipment and components we needed, take out our personal credit cards, and order what we needed through eBay so we would know the stuff would be there on Monday. Then we could start tinkering with the components and meet our deadline. Why our own credit cards? Because our company's internal systems would never work fast enough to help us out. We knew that if we got a patent out of it, nobody was going to yell at us for having used our personal cards!" He didn't wait for the procedures and processes; he disrupted them to help his company get farther, faster.

---

6   Marcus Buckingham and Curt Coffman, *First, Break All the Rules: What the World's Greatest Managers Do Differently* (New York: Simon & Schuster, 1999).

TAKE A BIG IDEA AND RIGHTSIZE IT

Earlier in this book, there was a reference to the Department of Defense and its 1,000-plus-page procurement manual. Greg Tennyson has a much smaller manual but still faces the challenge of getting employees to follow policy in the vision-care company where he is chief procurement officer. It's too small a project for an investment in artificial intelligence, so Greg took a different route. He worked with the marketing department to make entertaining videos to educate and remind employees about company policy. They created a character called Moolah who appears in short clips that pop up on people's laptops when they log in. There's a Moolah video about following the travel guidelines, another one about negotiating contracts, and others. They're all tiny reminders that are funny and unexpected, and they remind employees about the behaviors they're supposed to follow. It's a very simple, clever idea that can transfer to any industry and company. Something that humorous is the last thing you'd expect to pop up on your computer, but when it does, you pay attention—and maybe change your habits.

Imogen Heap is a musical artist based in the UK who has taken on the issue of fair payments getting back to the people who contribute to the music process. One of her songs is the first ever to use blockchain technology "to automatically distribute payments via a smart contract to all creatives involved in the making and recording of the song."[7] In other words, when we pay for her music, she uses the blockchain to distribute royalties and payments to all the people behind the scenes who are owed money—proof that a single person can still create Positive Disruption on a small scale.

And across the country, blockchain experiments are taking place in individual, modest-sized apartment buildings, testing the use of the technology to allow the sale of fractional shares to small investors and to facilitate the safe storage of data. One building at a time.

As you can see, you don't have to have the resources of an IBM or a Walmart to create a little disruption of your own. But you do need an idea.

WHERE TO START

Here's how you can start to initiate Positive Disruption:

- **Simplify.** Look at the processes you follow at work every day. Are they needed? What can you just stop doing? When you arrive at a new job, make a list of things you see that are cumbersome or outdated, or that just plain bother you. If you wait too long, you'll acclimate to these poorly designed systems and forget

---

7   Imogen Heap, "Blockchain Could Help Musicians Make Money Again," *Harvard Business Review*, June 5, 2017.

that they're inefficient. Take notes while you're new and able to see them objectively. If you've been with a company for a while, try to see the procedures and processes with fresh eyes. What makes people frustrated? What could be smoother and more efficient? Where are the bottlenecks?

- **Look for processes where there is no gatekeeper.** Someone in Department A does something and then passes it to someone in Department B, who adds information or makes changes and passes it on again. People are responsible for individual actions; no one is responsible for the whole flow end to end. A process without an owner is a perfect candidate for optimization or elimination. That express mail example just mentioned is a perfect situation where there was no gatekeeper, people just express-mailed documents to each other all day because that is how they moved paper. Few companies watch that kind of expense carefully. It took someone committed to positive improvement to question the effort, expense, and sense when the two companies were physically located only a few blocks apart.

- **Get to know an engineer.** Engineers know how to think. They know how to analyze and troubleshoot problems. Bounce ideas off each other—collaborate. Think about how you could change the process to make it easier, faster, or less error-prone. Consider how the process could be disrupted to make employees and customers happier.

- **Try a new technology.** No, your company isn't too small. There are lots of start-up companies developing apps or disruptive technologies, and some of them need clients to help them develop their products. Maybe your business can be a beta-test site, or work out a trial deal to test something for a while before you have to pay for it. At nearly every professional conference, there are companies displaying their services or technology. Don't bypass the "Solutions Zone" or whatever it's called in your industry. Talk to the companies; you'll be surprised how much they will help you.

- **Look around.** Get to know the people in other departments, and learn how you can leverage your own department's knowledge to help them and how they can help you. You may know things about internal processes or outside suppliers that help marketing achieve its goals faster or more efficiently, and the salespeople might be aware of a high demand that isn't being met by production. The sales department might be burdened with outdated software and processes, while the engineering department is humming along because that's the department that gets the attention when it comes to changing processes and technologies. Look around your company, and look outside your company, too. Read the business news, and see what the analysts are saying about the firm or the industry. What change can you help make that will create positive buzz?

- **Become "digitally savvy."** Chris Sawchuk used these words at a conference in 2016, and they become more relevant every day. You don't have to understand how to code, and you don't have to know how to build a computer, but you do need to have an appreciation for the fact that there is an ever-expanding number of ways in which an app, a piece of software, or a machine can help solve the problem at hand. The big picture here is that in order to disrupt, you need to get into a habit of actively listening and learning. What are people frustrated with? What are their gripes? Get together with your engineer friend and actually figure out how to make change. Make a small change in your own department, and see how it works out. Don't think that your company doesn't need disruption, because no entity does everything perfectly. Situations change, economies change, leadership changes, and customers change. Be the person who helps the company catch up to those changes. The results might astonish you. And at the very least, if things don't work out at your current company, you'll have something interesting to put on your résumé—something that will help you stand apart from *your* competition if you find yourself in the job market.

FIVE MINUTES AT A TIME

Not enough time? Try the "Five-Minute Rule." Set a goal

of five minutes a day, thirty minutes a week. (Take Sunday off.) You can read an article before you go to sleep instead of checking Facebook to troll your kids. Once a week, you can grab a salad and listen to one of those webinars constantly being offered for free while you eat lunch. You can listen to a podcast while you're driving. In my own specialty, Philip Ideson's *The Art of Procurement* offers podcasts for free on topics related to procurement and supply chain. What a great way to hear what successful disruptors are doing, and you can listen in small bits as time permits. There are hundreds of ways you can get exposure to new ideas, one paragraph at a time, five minutes at a time.

MAKE A NEW FRIEND IN A NEW BUSINESS

Who do you know? Who do you go to for ideas?

I was teaching a class on disruption to a bunch of smart, assertive people. But 75 percent of the class worked in the same industry, in the same city. Many of them were in the same company. They were all members of the same organization. How much debate do you think there was? How many new ideas? Not many—and most of them came from the 25 percent of the class that didn't already know each other.

People may change jobs, positions, and companies, but

they often move within the same circles. Part of this is geographic. Connecticut has a big insurance industry. New York contains a concentration of financial services firms. In California, it's technology, and in Boston, bio-tech. With that approach, you might become an expert in that industry, but your knowledge base can become very insular. The downside of employees sticking to one industry is that they don't get exposure to disruptive ideas or thinking from people in other industries, and those industries may offer great opportunities to learn.

Here's an example of where branching out worked well. One of the big, global ice cream brands started as a small, mom-and-pop business. As it grew, it made lots of batches of ice cream. One of the managers went on a tour of a beverage factory and saw that the flavors and materials arrived in large packages—big drums instead of small boxes. He brought that idea back, and the company saved money, spent less on freight, reduced the space it needed, and wasted a lot less packaging material—a positive success in every metric, because someone kept his eyes open for things that other people were doing differently than his company.

In the work I've been doing, I see a bit of a divide between businesses—almost a coastal divide. Lots of established companies are struggling to protect margins and continue to grow mature businesses, while the supply-chain professionals I meet in newer firms have a different set of problems. They're in start-up mode, trying to create a way to add value for the firms in which they work. They're newer, which means they don't have to deal with that legacy investment I was talking about earlier, but sooner or later, nearly all will face the margin squeeze of their more established counterparts.

If you're working in a situation like this, why not find someone in a different industry and ask them for their advice? What are their problems, and what are they doing to surmount them? Which of *your* problems have *they* already solved? Which of theirs have you solved? What is "different" in their firm—what kind of Positive Disruption is adding value or making employees' work lives easier? And how can you help them?

For example, businesses that rely on cold weather (like ski resorts) take out insurance to safeguard against the effects of winters that are too warm. If you're working for a company in the snowbelt, why not follow their lead and do the reverse? Consider insurance against the effects of a winter where the snowfall is higher than the norm, where you may get clobbered with snow removal costs. How can you use this idea if you are in any weather-dependent business?

Break out of your mold. Go to conferences that expose

you to different people, cultures, and ideas. Learn about other industries in other places and about different kinds of problems from the ones you deal with in your industry. Get to know people in a different box from the one you're in. If you're only attending the same seminars as everyone else and reading the same books and articles as others, then you're never going to have a big new idea. Push yourself, educate yourself, experiment, and reach out in ways you probably never expected.

Can't afford it? Volunteer to speak, participate in a panel discussion, or assist in some way, and most conference organizers will pay your expenses.

You shouldn't feel pressured to come up with groundbreaking, original ideas that nobody ever thought of before. The phrase "Any good idea is worth borrowing" has been used so many times that I can't figure out to whom the quote should be attributed, but it remains as true today as it was whenever it was first said.

KEY POINTS

- It's fun and fulfilling to be a change agent, a positive disruptor. You bring favorable benefits to the company you are working for now and create a way to set yourself apart if you're ever in the job market.

- Look outside your specialty, your industry, your geography. There's a lot of positive change out there. Learn what's happening at other companies and in other industries, and think about how you can adapt it to your company's situation.

- Don't be dissuaded by the scale of your idea. "Big ideas" are phenomenal. But small disruptions are good, too, and a few of these can help create a culture of Positive Disruption. Good results feed upon themselves and create even more positive changes.

QUESTIONS FOR THE READER

1. Look around you. What do you see that doesn't make sense? What can your company stop doing? What process or technology in your current company could be replaced, improved, or removed?

2. What new idea—large or small—can you bring forward?

3. What can you do personally to learn more about disruptive businesses or technologies that might be transferable to your employer?

CHAPTER SEVEN

THE LAST PIECE OF THE PUZZLE

I took a machine-design class once where it seemed like all we did was calculus. Week after week. Most of the class was mystified, myself included.

Then it all came together. The last few sessions, the professor combined all the elements, and it made perfect sense.

That's our task now. We began with a story about a toolkit at the start of Chapter One, and now, we end with a reminder about the concepts you've learned—the tools you'll develop, sharpen, and maintain over the years.

As a result of workplace disruption, you'll probably find yourself at a crossroads multiple times in your career.

Circumstances will oblige you to make changes, whether you want to or not. The skills in this book, and everything you learn on the job, are transferable even when tangible items from your old jobs aren't. You won't be able to take your old laptop with you when you leave a company, but you will be able to take your knowledge and the experience you gained putting the ideas in this book into practice.

On a personal level, figure out what you need to do to deal with the churn in your industry, your workplace. Even if you're right out of school with complete flexibility to move as you need to, sooner or later, you'll have commitments and relationships that make you less able to weather the ups and downs of your work life—unless you have a plan. Not just a financial plan but also one that ensures you stay visible, relevant, and sought after. Simple as that.

Begin taking time to gain an understanding of your own personality and preferences, and those of the people with whom you come into contact. Create strategies for how you interact with others, and adjust your actions and reactions accordingly. Do what's necessary, not what comes naturally. Remember that every interaction and conversation is a type of negotiation, but don't be afraid if you don't naturally think well on your feet. Compensate by learning the basic elements of negotiation and being well prepared.

Get out from behind your desk. Since churn is likely to

take you into other companies, it will always pay to be creating networks in various industries as you go along. Make contacts outside your current industry and geography. Meet people who do your job at another firm, and learn about their challenges. Pull something from that person or field that will help you in your current job. The opportunities that spring from active and constant networking are endless. Every industry is evolving, and you never know what changes are coming.

Then, practice Positive Disruption.

Make good things happen by bringing ideas to your workplace, large or small. Embrace change.

- Think about the things in your current role or company that don't work well.
- Educate yourself on positive changes that are taking place in other companies and other industries.
- Look for ways to adapt other ideas if you can't think of a solution yourself.
- Sell your ideas by learning a few negotiating techniques and adapting your message to the styles of the people you need to persuade.
- Do your homework. You don't have to be a genius if you are well prepared.

Positive Disruption is rewarding. It makes you feel like

you've really accomplished something. And it helps you stand apart from the crowd.

Ideas evolve. Forty years ago, I couldn't have written this book, because I couldn't foresee what was ahead. Disruption wasn't covered in any college curriculum. Personal computers didn't exist, and we weren't worried about jobs moving offshore or disappearing entirely as technology replaced people. The role models I had, the exposures to churn and disruption—all happened over time and resulted in the development of these suggestions.

If you're just starting your career, you've only had a few opportunities to make yourself stand apart. If you're a new parent, you have limited time to spare. If you've just bought a place to live or are paying off student loans, you are living with a tight budget. So you start small, keeping the end goal in mind. A few of you may be able to do all of this at once, but by and large, you can pick from the suggestions in this book and start with a handful of them.

Thriving in today's corporate world doesn't have to be a battle. Once you understand yourself and the world you're in and are willing to make some adjustments to adapt, you can make a positive impact and have a good time in the process.

No job, no company, no process is perfect. But you can

make it better. Thomas Edison said, "To invent, you need a good imagination and a pile of junk." You don't have to be a scientist or technology genius. You just need the will to make things better, an inquiring mind, and a handful of tools.

I hope you will use lessons from this book as a guide to navigating the changing waters of work. Embrace the churn, and make Positive Disruption work for you.

ACKNOWLEDGMENTS

Thank you, first and foremost, to the disruptors out there. Whether you're starting a company or making great changes where you work today, the world needs you.

I struggle mightily with writer's block and, after a year on the book, had only an outline and a few pages of work to show for my efforts. Thank you, Rob Karp, for suggesting Scribe Media, where Tucker Max, Kathleen Pederson, Kevin Murphy, Susan Paul, Zach Obront, and Diana Fitts helped me find my voice and get it better organized than I ever could have done without their help.

To Amaris Sicklick and Samantha Rayward at City Headshots. You are miracle workers.

To Frank Musero and the WBResearch ProcureCon team,

thank you for consistently allowing me to try out my ideas by speaking at their excellent conferences. And to Carina Kuhl, Frank's predecessor, for the same.

To Kevin Rohan, one of the USA's foremost procurement/supply chain recruiters. First, thank you for helping me staff organizations multiple times when business churn of one sort or another created the need for a team; and for also being willing to share your observations on trends and trendsetters to help me ensure my teams and I were incorporating new thinking into our work.

To Kelly Barner and Philip Ideson, two of the world's greatest collaborators. Thank you immensely for your brains, your input, your ideas, and your time. You are both the epitome of positive disruption.

To the bosses who took chances on me: Brian McGrath, Jesse Penn, Sara Douglass, Larry Henriques, Jim Litts, Art Vitarius, Nello Trevison, Jerry Lieberman, and Bob Rozek. Thank you for the opportunities to try new things and to have the experiences that brought me here.

To the folks who took even bigger chances on me as I morphed from being an executive to an independent agent. To Sarika Garaug and Vishal Patel at Tradeshift. To Tiza Peterson, Abby Wadsworth, Jon Ollinger, Brooke Dito, Mel Ohl, Julienne Ryan, Christoph Kienzel, and the already mentioned Frank Musero. To Craig Cuyar, thanks for the coaching.

Stephany Lapierre, Stan Garber, Nick Ammaturo, and Christian Lanng—you are all disruptors I admire.

There have been some larger-than-life people on the teams I've managed. They made every day disruptive, in a good way. Thank you, Richard Porcaro, Connie Mammone, Rick Thielen, Jeff Haye, Art Brunton, Tandra Davis, John Weidner, Chuck Mihalik, Barbara Donnelly, Victoria Moore, and Claudia Hurtado.

Chris Sawchuk is a respected expert in the Supply Chain Space, who has a calendar that's booked solid and lots of big names vying for his attention, yet he made time for me more than once, providing ideas and suggestions each time I found myself needing outside advice. Thank you, Chris, and thank you, Diane Banhidi.

Paul Smith, a successful author himself, gave me the lay of the land as I was beginning this process. Thank you, Paul, for your honest recounting of your own experience and for your encouragement.

A salute to Aggie Hanczewski, Mireia Brancos, Casey Scott, and Mariel Antesberger. I've had the pleasure of mentoring you a bit and learning from you a lot. Thank you immensely for being so brilliant. You have bright futures and you're already such good role models for the generations coming behind you.

Thank you to my sister, Janice Vogel, and godson, Mark Vogel—your good questions about my elevator speech made me take a critical look at the draft of this book. It was all wrong, and I wouldn't have rewritten it (twice) if we hadn't "talked business" one afternoon.

To Christopher Alesevich, Michael Torre, Scott Martinez, and Devra Glauberman Martinez. You provided information and perspectives from the viewpoints of your generation, allowing this book to reflect broader ideas than just my own.

Thank you to the friends who encouraged me: the Walkers, Ghis Palumbo, Miss Chris, Montse, Pat Bender, Em and Bill, AMK, and Basia. You were patient when I spoke endlessly about the process of creating the book, and I am eternally grateful for your interest and support. Sophie and Chet, I know that you feel the same. Natalia too.

Finally, to my family, who gives me more joy and inspiration than can be described.

To Christina, William, and Scott. My heart bursts with pride at the three of you. You experienced the good and the bad of having a mom who worked outside the home. Today you are smart, curious, adaptable "citizens of the world," influenced, at least a bit, by the experiences you were able to have as a result of our family adventures. Brian, Dev, and Barb—you are wonderful additions to the team. I love you all.

To Olivia, Ella, Wyatt, Westin, and the babies to come. People do all kinds of things when they stop working for a company and start working for themselves. JoNana wrote this book. You've already been such immensely positive disruptors in our lives. If I'm gone by the time you are old enough to read this, remember my advice: *"Embrace the Churn."*

Big hugs to Will Martinez. Thank you for telling Alexa to be quiet when I needed to concentrate. This process was much longer than you or I ever imagined, and I appreciate your encouragement, patience, and not rolling your eyeballs too much when I'd tell people I was almost done. Let's start packing...I'll go on that cruise with you now.

JOANNA MARTINEZ

2018

ABOUT THE AUTHOR

 In a career spanning four decades, corporate executive **JOANNA MARTINEZ** led transformation initiatives of various types within Johnson & Johnson, Diageo, AllianceBernstein LP, and Cushman & Wakefield. Today, as founder of Supply Chain Advisors LLC, her clients range from start-ups and professional organizations to Fortune 500 companies.

Joanna is a noted speaker and thought leader on global procurement and supply chain topics and works as a consultant, advisor, and coach. Twice designated a "Pro to Know," she was named a Distinguished Alumna by Rutgers College of Engineering, where she sits on the school's Industry Advisory Board. Joanna has been recognized by multiple organizations for innovation or customer excellence.

Manufactured by Amazon.ca
Bolton, ON

10434523R00088